At Issue

WITHDRAWN

Gay Marriage

Other Books in the At Issue Series:

Contents

Introduction

The issue of gay, or same-sex, marriage has become one of the most polarizing public policy matters in American politics. Gay rights advocates see it as one of the gay movement's main goals and argue that gay Americans have a right as citizens to express love and commitment through marriage, as well as a right to its many legal benefits. Gay marriage opponents, who tend to be religious groups and political conservatives, see marriage as limited to one man and one woman and think that allowing same-sex couples to marry would undermine that institution. Although most states have shown no interest in approving gay marriage, and about 41 explicitly ban it, a handful of states now allow same-sex marriages—including Washington DC, Connecticut, Iowa, Massachusetts, New Hampshire, Vermont, and most recently, New York. Other states are still enmeshed in political and legal disputes over the gay marriage issue. The most notable example of this is California, where the state supreme court in 2008 ruled a ban on gay marriage unconstitutional but voters then restored the ban in a ballot measure called Proposition 8. Litigation challenging Proposition 8, many legal experts believe, could end up before the US Supreme Court.

The California same-sex marriage battle began on May 15, 2008, when the Supreme Court of California in a case called *In re Marriage Cases* ruled that the California constitution protects same-sex marriage and that a state law banning it constituted illegal discrimination. Outraged by the decision, gay marriage opponents launched a campaign to put a referendum—Proposition 8 (commonly referred to as Prop 8)—on the November 2008 ballot, asking California voters to once again ban same-sex marriage. Proposition 8 passed on November 4, 2008 by a 52.3 to 47.7 percent margin. The very next day, three lawsuits were filed with the California Supreme

Court challenging the legality of Proposition 8. The lawsuits argued that Prop 8 was technically invalid because it was a substantive revision rather than an amendment to the California constitution, and because revisions require action by the legislature before they can be placed before voters. The state supreme court agreed to hear the cases, but on May 26, 2009 upheld Prop 8. At the same time, the court ruled that an estimated 18,000 gay couples who married before the proposition took effect could stay legally married.

Shortly before the California Supreme Court ruling on Prop 8, however, a pro-gay-marriage group, the American Foundation for Equal Rights (AFER), filed suit in federal court challenging Prop 8's ban on same-sex marriage. Attorneys for AFER included David Boies and Theodore Olson—two men who had worked on opposing sides in the landmark *Bush v. Gore* case before the US Supreme Court that resolved the dispute over the 2000 presidential election results. Although Boies is a prominent liberal and Olson a well-known conservative who served as Solicitor General during Republican George W. Bush's administration, they agree that the right to marry is a fundamental right guaranteed by the US Constitution and thus a right that cannot be denied to gay couples. Their lawsuit, in the case called *Perry v. Schwarzenegger*, made these arguments before federal district court judge Vaughn Walker on June 16, 2010.

Weeks later, on August 4, 2010, Judge Walker issued his ruling, overturning Prop 8. Walker concluded that the proposition's gay marriage ban was unconstitutional under the Due Process and Equal Protection clauses of the US Constitution because California had no good reason for denying gays and lesbians a fundamental right—the right to marry. In his opinion, Judge Walker explained that a heightened legal standard, called strict scrutiny, should apply because gays and lesbians are exactly the type of minority that the standard was designed to protect. However, Walker found that the gay marriage ban could not even pass muster under a lesser legal standard known as rational basis, which simply requires that an action be rationally related to legitimate government purpose. As Walker said in his 138-page opinion, the anti-gay-marriage supporters "failed to build a credible factual record to support their claim that Proposition 8 served a legitimate government interest."[1] Instead, Walker said that the facts—including that marriage is a civil rather than a religious matter; that people do not choose their sexual orientation and cannot change it; that gays and lesbians have a long history as victims of discrimination; and that sexual orientation does not prevent a person from being a good parent—supported judgment in favor of the AFER attorneys. Gay marriage opponents appealed Judge Walker's decision to the federal Ninth Circuit Court of Appeals.

To rule on the *Perry v. Schwarzenegger* case the federal appeals court had to determine whether the supporters of Prop 8 have standing—that is, the legal right to appeal Judge Walker's ruling. This issue arose because California Governor Jerry Brown and state Attorney General Kamala D. Harris refused to appeal or defend Prop 8, leaving only the referendum's sponsors as the appellants. Since the appellate court's analysis involved interpreting California law, the court asked the California Supreme Court to rule on the question of standing. Accordingly, the state supreme court heard arguments on this question on September 6, 2011, and on November 17, 2011 the court ruled that Prop 8 proponents had legal standing.

After hearing arguments, the Ninth Circuit Court of Appeals issued a 2-to-1 majority opinion on February 7, 2012 that upheld Judge Walkers's 2010 ruling that Prop 8 is unconstitutional. Writing for the majority, Judge Stephen Reinhardt stated:

1. *Perry v. Schwarzenegger*, No. C 09-2292 VRW (N.D. CA August 4, 2010). www.sfgate.com.

Prior to November 4, 2008, the California Constitution guaranteed the right to marry to opposite-sex couples and same-sex couples alike. On that day, the People of California adopted Proposition 8, which amended the state constitution to eliminate the right of same-sex couples to marry. We consider whether that amendment violates the Fourteenth Amendment to the United States Constitution. We conclude that it does.

Although the Constitution permits communities to enact most laws they believe to be desirable, it requires that there be at least a legitimate reason for the passage of a law that treats different classes of people differently. There was no such reason that Proposition 8 could have been enacted. Because under California statutory law, same-sex couples had all the rights of opposite-sex couples, regardless of their marital status, all parties agree that Proposition 8 had one effect only. It stripped same-sex couples of the ability they previously possessed to obtain from the State, or any other authorized party, an important right—the right to obtain and use the designation of 'marriage' to describe their relationships. Nothing more, nothing less. Proposition 8 therefore could not have been enacted to advance California's interests in childrearing or responsible procreation, for it had no effect on the rights of same-sex couples to raise children or on the procreative practices of other couples. Nor did Proposition 8 have any effect on religious freedom or on parents' rights to control their children's education; it could not have been enacted to safeguard these liberties.

All that Proposition 8 accomplished was to take away from same-sex couples the right to be granted marriage licenses and thus legally to use the designation of 'marriage,' which symbolizes state legitimization and societal recognition of their committed relationships. Proposition 8 serves no purpose, and has no effect, other than to lessen the status and human dignity of gays and lesbians in California, and to reclassify their relationships and families as inferior to those of opposite-sex couples. The Constitution simply does not allow for "laws of this sort."[2]

While this decision represented a major victory for gay-marriage advocates, the court also issued a stay on the decision, preventing gay marriages from taking place in California. On February 21, 2012, proponents of Prop 8 appealed the Ninth Circuit Court's judgment and requested a review of the case by the entire 11-member Circuit Court panel. If the court agrees to this review, it would delay review of the case by the US Supreme Court. Another way that the gay marriage issue could reach the US Supreme Court is through litigation on the constitutionality of the 1996 Defense of Marriage Act (DOMA), a federal law that defines marriage as only between a man and a woman. In February 2011, President Barack Obama directed the US Department of Justice to stop defending DOMA in the courts. At least two cases are now proceeding through the federal courts on the issue of whether DOMA's gay marriage ban is constitutional, and especially since there is a Ninth Circuit decision on gay marriage, the US Supreme Court could decide to take on the issue at some time in the not too distant future. Meanwhile, the debate about gay marriage continues. The authors of the viewpoints in *At Issue: Gay Marriage* present a number of key arguments made by supporters and opponents of same-sex marriage.

2. Judge Stephen Reinhardt, United States Court of Appeals for the Ninth Circuit, No. 10-16696, D.C. No. 3:09-cv-02292-VRW, Opinion, Case No. 10-16696, filed February 7, 2012.

1

Gay Marriage Should Be Legal

James Kellard

James Kellard is a writer of news articles, political analyses, and book and travel reviews.

The arguments against gay marriage do not hold up. Most of the anti-gay marriage arguments involve religion but conservatives should not be permitted to impose their religious ideas on others who do not share them or to deny civil marriage to homosexuals. Notably, conservatives do not argue that the US Constitution bans gay marriage, probably because the opposite is true: The 14th Amendment likely protects gay marriage. The new arguments that gay marriage might be discussed in schools or that gays should not be able to define marriage for heterosexuals are equally hollow. Children cannot be shielded from information that is widely available on television and elsewhere, and there is no reason religious groups should be allowed to define marriage for homosexuals.

The issue of gay marriage hit the national stage during the 2004 elections as a divisive issue meant to drive religious conservatives to the polls. Seven years later this issue has not gone away. While it is understandable that some may be uncomfortable with the idea of two people of the same sex getting married, the arguments against it are flimsy at best.

Protecting the Institution of Marriage

The most common argument against allowing gays to marry seems to be that we need to protect the institution of mar-

At Issue

|Gay Marriage

Debra A. Miller, Book Editor

GREENHAVEN PRESS
A part of Gale, Cengage Learning

 GALE
CENGAGE Learning·

Detroit • New York • San Francisco • New Haven, Conn • Waterville, Maine • London

Elizabeth Des Chenes, *Director, Publishing Solutions*

For more information, contact:
Greenhaven Press
27500 Drake Rd.
Farmington Hills, MI 48331-3535
Or you can visit our Internet site at gale.cengage.com

Articles in Greenhaven Press anthologies are often edited for length to meet page requirements. In addition, original titles of these works are changed to clearly present the main thesis and to explicitly indicate the author's opinion. Every effort is made to ensure that Greenhaven Press accurately reflects the original intent of the authors. Every effort has been made to trace the owners of copyrighted material.

LIBRARY OF CONGRESS CATALOGING-IN-PUBLICATION DATA

Gay marriage / Debra A. Miller, book editor.
    p. cm. -- (At issue)
    Includes bibliographical references and index.
    ISBN 978-0-7377-5894-8 (hbk.) -- ISBN 978-0-7377-5895-5 (pbk.)
    1. Same-sex marriage--United States. I. Miller, Debra A.
    HQ1034.U5G393 2011
    306.84'80973--dc23

                                                              2011044644

Printed in the United States of America
    1 2 3 4 5   16 15 14 13 12

FD135

riage. This argument is ridiculous for many reasons. While the main reason people in the US seem to get married is out of love, it is by no means the only reason.

There are people who marry for money, non-sexual companionship, even health insurance, do these reasons also threaten the institution of marriage? Furthermore, we have to look at marriage historically. For many years a wife was considered the property of her husband. For generations, royal families would marry their children off for diplomatic reasons, even "lower class" families would marry their daughters off to wealthy and/or powerful families so that they may reap the benefits. Many countries still have arranged marriages. Call me crazy but it appears that marriage is not exactly as "sacred" an institution as some would like to think.

Of course what makes the "protecting the institution of marriage" argument so ridiculous is that the divorce rate in the US is now over 50 percent. If we really want to protect marriage shouldn't we outlaw divorce? Finally, it is extremely difficult to comprehend how a gay couple getting married will effect heterosexual marriages. Will homosexuals getting married be so stressful to heterosexuals that we will all have break downs and divorce our wives and husbands?

It seems absurd to even suggest that it would be more beneficial for a child to be raised in an abusive home over that of a loving same sex couple.

Protecting Children

Another argument against same sex marriage is that we need to "protect" our children. Are we worried that letting gays get married will double the attendance of the conversion parties to turn all our children gay? If we are talking about the children of a gay couple whether through adoption (that is a whole other issue), artificial insemination, surrogacy, or the old fashioned way; then would it not be more beneficial for these children to have a married couple as parents, particularly for legal reasons?

Some may say that the "ideal" situation for children to be raised in is with a loving mother and father. While this may not be wrong, it is not reality. It would be great if everyone had a loving mother and father, but how many children are being raised by single parents because one parent took off, or have a mother and father but are neglected or abused? It seems absurd to even suggest that it would be more beneficial for a child to be raised in an abusive home over that of a loving same sex couple.

Religion

Practically all of the arguments against gay marriage come back to the issue of religion. Many extremely religious conservatives like to remind us that there is freedom of religion in this country, but some do not seem to understand that freedom of religion does not mean everybody conforming to your own personal religious beliefs. Some will say that since gay marriage is against their religious beliefs it is a violation of their freedom of religion.

There is no constitutional basis for denying marriage rights to same sex couples, if anything the opposite is true.

The same argument can be made for homosexuals though. Since the beliefs of religious conservatives (generally) are not their beliefs, doesn't that violate homosexuals' freedom of religion? We are all entitled to our own beliefs, but we should not expect everybody else to conform to them. Same sex marriage has no logical impact on the everyday lives of religious conservatives, but religious conservatives denying same sex couples the right to marry does have a direct impact on the everyday lives of homosexuals.

Marriage may be a religious issue for many but the fact is, we also have civil marriage, which has absolutely nothing to do with religion. Religious groups and churches have every right to deny same sex marriage in their parish, but they have absolutely no right to deny it in city hall.

There is a huge uproar if someone who may be Muslim even considers running for office, the most common reason given appears to be that many do not want the Muslim beliefs pushed onto them. That is a perfectly valid expectation, but we should all abide by the same rules. No matter what our religion, we should practice all we want, but we have no right to expect that others should live by our beliefs. Most importantly, religion, whether it is Catholicism, Christianity, Judaism, Hinduism, etc, has absolutely no place in government. None of us have a monopoly on morality.

No Constitutional Basis for Banning Gay Marriage

Interestingly, you rarely hear an argument against same sex marriage citing the Constitution to reinforce their argument. This is because there is no constitutional basis for denying marriage rights to same sex couples, if anything the opposite is true.

Section 1 of the 14th Amendment to the Constitution reads as follows:

> "All persons born or naturalized in the United States, and subject to the jurisdiction thereof, are citizens of the United States and of the state wherein they reside. No state shall make or enforce any law which shall abridge the privileges or immunities of citizens of the United States; nor shall any state deprive any person of life, liberty, or property, without due process of law; nor deny to any person within its jurisdiction the equal protection of the laws."

Seems pretty clear cut. Some argue that nowhere in the Constitution does it specifically mention anything about same

15

sex marriage. This argument is flimsy at best and barely merits acknowledgement. What is very clearly stated is ". . . citizens of the United States." Homosexuals and lesbians are tax-paying, law abiding citizens and deserve the same rights and legal protections as every other citizen of the United States.

The most recent, highly publicized legal challenge to proponents of gay marriage, was in 2008 with Proposition 8 in California. What was so controversial about this was that the California Supreme Court had already ruled that same sex couples had a constitutional right to marry. Proposition 8 stripped away rights that same sex couples already had. The arguments in favor of "Prop 8" were the same recycled arguments; protecting the institution of marriage, protecting the very fabric of society (with a 50+% divorce rate), and of course, "protecting" the children.

New Arguments

Apparently most of the other arguments have been losing steam, so the newest was that allowing gays to marry would cause public schools to teach that gay marriage is "okay."

I suppose I must have missed the "marriage class" in elementary school. The only way this topic could possibly come up is if one or more of the children are directly affected by it, such as if they have same sex parents, or other family members in same sex relationships. Using the logic of not teaching children that gay marriage is okay, the only alternative would be to chastise the child for bringing it up, and informing the rest of the class that this is not "okay" and there is something wrong with this child's parents and/or family members. I cannot begin to understand how this would be more beneficial for children.

Of course there is always the possibility that the topic of gay marriage may come up in class because of outside influences such as a child hearing about it at home or seeing it on television. This would seem impossible though, if the same parents who do not want their children learning about this issue at school are monitoring them at home, they should never have the opportunity to hear about it. This logic also brings up the question, is it ever right to bring this topic up with your children? It is understandable that it would be difficult to discuss the issue of same sex marriage with a six year old, but what about when they are ten, twelve, sixteen, is it more beneficial to monitor every aspect of their life until they are eighteen to make sure that nobody, at any time, ever brings up the topic of gay marriage? If the goal of raising a child is to completely shelter them from anything that may contradict your own personal beliefs, would it not be better to home-school them?

A second "new argument" that started to emerge a bit more during the Proposition 8 debate, was a simple question, "Why should gay people and special rights groups be allowed to redefine marriage for the rest of us?" The obvious counter question would be, "Why should religious and special rights groups be allowed to define marriage for homosexuals?" What makes one group better than the other? Furthermore, which definition of marriage are we using? The one where a wife is the property of her husband and it is legal to beat her? Or arranging marriages based on social status? Should interracial marriage be illegal again as it was for almost two centuries? Perhaps it is time to draft separate "partnership licenses" to those who are marrying only for money, or is that still included under this definition of marriage? Obviously marriage has been redefined many times.

The People Versus the Courts

After Proposition 8 passed, proponents argued that it would be wrong to fight the decision because it was decided by the people rather than by the courts. While we are a democracy, we are also a country that was assembled for the very purpose of protecting all American citizens despite their opinion, belief, or lifestyle. Obviously we don't always get it right the first time as it took generations to abolish slavery, allow women the right to vote, allow black and white children to attend school together, and allow interracial marriage, historically no matter how long it takes, we as a country always end up choosing freedom over oppression. Of course there are always those fighting against it, and if you look back the argument is always the same, that it will be the destruction of our society. Somehow though, we always seem to survive it and become a better country because of it.

The whole argument really comes down to letting consenting adults do as they wish, provided they are not hurting anybody, and keeping our beliefs out of the lives of others, just as we expect for ourselves. Homosexuals getting married really has no effect on anybody but themselves. Although with all the extra weddings, gifts, and honeymoons, it would actually be a good way to stimulate the economy!

2

Gay Marriage Should Not Be Legal

Peter Sprigg

Peter Sprigg is Senior Fellow for Policy Studies at the Family Research Council, a non-profit organization that advocates for faith, family, and freedom in public policy and public opinion.

Supporters of gay marriage claim it will not hurt anyone, but there would be both immediate and long-term harms that would come from legalizing same sex marriage. Among the immediate effects would be taxpayer subsidies to homosexuals, including Social Security benefits, the teaching of homosexual values in public schools, and threats to religious liberty when churches and religious institutions are challenged not to discriminate against gays. Longer-term effects would include fewer people marrying, fewer sexually faithful relationships, more divorces, fewer children being raised by both a mother and a father, a falling birth rate, and demands for recognition of polygamy as a legitimate form of marriage.

Some advocates of same-sex "marriage" scoff at the idea that it could harm anyone. Here are ten ways in which society could be harmed by legalizing same-sex "marriage." Most of these effects would become evident only in the long run, but several would occur immediately.

Taxpayers, Consumers, and Businesses Would Be Forced to Subsidize Homosexual Relationships

One of the key arguments often heard in support of homosexual civil "marriage" revolves around all the government "benefits" that homosexuals claim they are denied. Many of these "benefits" involve one thing—taxpayer money that homosexuals are eager to get their hands on. For example, one of the goals of homosexual activists is to take part in the biggest government entitlement program of all—Social Security. Homosexuals want their partners to be eligible for Social Security survivors benefits when one partner dies.

The fact that Social Security survivors benefits were intended to help stay-at-home mothers who did not have retirement benefits from a former employer has not kept homosexuals from demanding the benefit. Homosexual activists are also demanding that children raised by a homosexual couple be eligible for benefits when one of the partners dies—even if the deceased partner was not the child's biological or adoptive parent.

One of the goals of homosexual activists is to take part in the biggest government entitlement program of all— Social Security.

As another example, homosexuals who are employed by the government want to be able to name their homosexual partners as dependents in order to get the taxpayers to pay for health insurance for them. Never mind that most homosexual couples include two wage-earners, each of whom can obtain their own insurance. Never mind that "dependents" were, when the tax code was developed, assumed to be children and stay-at-home mothers. And never mind that homosexuals have higher rates of physical disease, mental illness, and substance abuse, leading to more medical claims and higher insurance premiums. No, all of these logical considerations must give way in the face of the demand for taxpayer subsidies of homosexual relationships.

But these costs would be imposed not only upon governments, but upon businesses and private organizations as well. Some organizations already offer "domestic partner" benefits to same-sex couples as a matter of choice. Social conservatives have discouraged such policies, but we have not attempted to forbid them by law.

Imagine, though, what the impact on employee benefit programs would be if homosexual "marriage" is legalized nationwide. Right now, marriage still provides a clear, bright line, both legally and socially, to distinguish those who receive dependent benefits and those who don't. But if homosexual couples are granted the full legal status of civil "marriage," then employers who do not want to grant benefits to homosexual partners—whether out of principle, or simply because of a prudent economic judgment—would undoubtedly be coerced by court orders to do so.

Another important and immediate result of same-sex "marriage" would be serious damage to religious liberty.

Schools Would Teach That Homosexual Relationships Are Identical to Heterosexual Ones

The advocates of same-sex "marriage" argue that it will have little impact on anyone other than the couples who "marry." However, even the brief experience in Massachusetts, where same-sex "marriage" was imposed by the state's Supreme Judicial Court and began on May 17, 2004, has demonstrated that the impact of such a social revolution will extend much further—including into the public schools. In September 2004,

National Public Radio reported, "Already, some gay and lesbian advocates are working on a new gay-friendly curriculum for kindergarten and up." They also featured an interview with Deb Allen, a lesbian who teaches eighth-grade sex education in Brookline, Mass. Allen now feels "emboldened" in teaching a "gay-friendly" curriculum, declaring, "If somebody wants to challenge me, I'll say, 'Give me a break. It's legal now.'" Her lessons include descriptions of homosexual sex given "thoroughly and explicitly with a chart." Allen reports she will ask her students, "Can a woman and a woman have vaginal intercourse, and they will all say no. And I'll say, 'Hold it. Of course, they can. They can use a sex toy. They could use'— and we talk—and we discuss that. So the answer there is yes." . . .

Freedom of Conscience and Religious Liberty Would Be Threatened

Another important and immediate result of same-sex "marriage" would be serious damage to religious liberty.

Religious liberty means much more than liturgical rituals. It applies not only to formal houses of worship, but to parachurch ministries, religious educational and social service organizations, and individual believers trying to live their lives in accordance with their faith not only at church, but at home, in their neighborhoods, and in the workplace. These, more than your pastor or parish priest, are the entities whose religious liberty is most threatened by same-sex "marriage."

Some of these threats to religious liberty can arise from "nondiscrimination" laws based on sexual orientation, even without same-sex "marriage." But when homosexual "marriage" becomes legal, then laws which once applied to homosexuals only as individuals then apply to homosexual couples as well. So, for example, when Catholic Charities in Boston insisted that they would stay true to principle and refuse to place children for adoption with same-sex couples, they were told by the state that they could no longer do adoptions at all.

In other cases, a variety of benefits or opportunities that the state makes available to religious nonprofits could be withheld based on the organization's refusal to treat same-sex couples and "marriages" the same as opposite-sex marriages. Organizations might be denied government grants or aid otherwise available to faith-based groups; they might be denied access to public facilities for events; and they might even have their tax-exempt status removed. That is what happened to the Ocean Grove Camp Meeting Association in New Jersey when they refused to rent facilities for a lesbian "civil union" ceremony.

Religious educational institutions are particularly at risk, because in some cases they may allow students who are not believers to attend and even have staff who are not adherents of their religion, but still desire to maintain certain religiously-informed norms and standards of behavior. Yet a Lutheran school in California has been sued for expelling two girls who were in a lesbian relationship. Yeshiva University, a Jewish school in New York City, was forced to allow same-sex "domestic partners" in married-student housing. Religious clubs on secular campuses may be denied recognition if they oppose homosexual conduct—this happened to the Christian Legal Society at the University of California's Hastings School of Law.

Professionals would face lawsuits or even a denial of licensing if they refuse to treat homosexual relationships the same as heterosexual ones. A California fertility doctor was sued for declining to artificially inseminate a lesbian woman. And the online dating service eHarmony succumbed to the pressure of a lawsuit and agreed to provide services for same-sex couples as well.

Individual believers who disapprove of homosexual relationships may be the most vulnerable of all, facing a choice at work between forfeiting their freedom of speech and being fired.

Religious liberty is one of the deepest American values. We must not sacrifice it on the altar of political correctness that homosexual "marriage" would create.

Fewer People Would Marry

Even where legal recognition and marital rights and benefits are available to same-sex couples (whether through same-sex civil "marriages," "civil unions," or "domestic partnerships"), *relatively few same-sex couples even bother to seek such recognition or claim such benefits.*

The most simple way to document this is by comparing the number of same-sex couples who have sought such legal recognition in a given state with the number of "same-sex unmarried-partner households" in the most recent U.S. Census.

When a relatively small percentage of same-sex couples—even among those already living together as partners—even bother to seek legal recognition of their relationships, while an overwhelming majority of heterosexual couples who live together are legally married, it suggests that homosexuals are far more likely than heterosexuals to *reject the institution of marriage* or its legal equivalent.

In California, same-sex "marriage" was only legal for a few months, from the time that the California Supreme Court ruled in May of 2008 until the voters adopted Proposition 8 in November of the same year. Press reports have indicated that about 18,000 same-sex couples got "married" in California—*less than 20% of the total* identified by the Census. By contrast, 91% of opposite-sex couples who lived together in California were married. In other words, only 9% of heterosexual couples in California have rejected the institution of marriage, while over 80% of the homosexual couples rejected "marriage" when it was offered to them in 2008. . . .

Couples who could marry, but choose instead to cohabit without the benefit of marriage, harm the institution of marriage by setting an example for other couples, making nonmarital cohabitation seem more acceptable as well. If same-sex "marriage" were legalized, the evidence suggests that the percentage of homosexual couples who would choose cohabitation over "marriage" would be much larger than the current percentage of heterosexual couples who choose cohabitation over marriage. It is likely that the poor example set by homosexual couples would, over time, lead to lower marriage rates among heterosexuals as well.

Fewer People Would Remain Monogamous and Sexually Faithful

One value that remains remarkably strong, even among people who have multiple sexual partners before marriage, is the belief that marriage itself is a sexually exclusive relationship. Among married heterosexuals, having sexual relations with anyone other than one's spouse is still considered a grave breach of trust and a violation of the marriage covenant by the vast majority of people.

Yet the same cannot be said of homosexuals—particularly of homosexual men. Numerous studies of homosexual relationships, including "partnered" relationships, covering a span of decades, have shown that sex with multiple partners is tolerated and often expected, even when one has a "long-term" partner. Perhaps the most startling of these studies was published in the journal *AIDS*. In the context of studying HIV risk behavior among young homosexual men in the Netherlands, the researchers found that homosexual men who were *in partnered relationships* had an *average* of eight sexual partners *per year* outside of the primary relationship. This is an astonishing contrast to the typical behavior of married heterosexuals, among whom 75% of the men and 85% of the women report *never* having had extra-marital sex even once during the entire duration of their marriage. . . .

Fewer People Would Remain Married for a Lifetime

Lawrence Kurdek, a homosexual psychologist from Ohio's Wright State University, who has done extensive research on the nature of homosexual relationships, has correctly stated, "Perhaps the most important 'bottom-line' question about gay and lesbian couples is whether their relationships last." After extensive research, he determined that "it is safe to conclude that gay and lesbian couples dissolve their relationships more frequently than heterosexual couples, especially heterosexual couples with children."

Society would be placing its highest stamp of official government approval on the deliberate creation of permanently motherless and fatherless households.

Once again, abundant research has borne out this point. Older studies came to similar conclusions. In one study of 156 male couples, for instance, only seven had been together for longer than five years. . . .

Fewer Children Would Be Raised by a Married Mother and Father

The greatest tragedy resulting from the legalization of homosexual "marriage" would not be its effect on adults, but its effect on children. For the first time in history, society would be placing its highest stamp of official government approval on the *deliberate* creation of *permanently* motherless or fatherless households for children.

There simply cannot be any serious debate, based on the mass of scholarly literature available to us, about the ideal family form for children. It consists of a mother and father who are committed to one another in marriage. Children raised by their married mother and father experience lower rates of many social pathologies, including:

- premarital childbearing;

- illicit drug use;

- arrest;

- health, emotional, or behavioral problems;

- poverty;

- or school failure or expulsion.

These benefits are then passed on to future generations as well, because children raised by their married mother and father are themselves less likely to cohabit or to divorce as adults.

In a perfect world, every child would have that kind of household provided by his or her own loving and capable biological parents (and every husband and wife who wanted children would be able to conceive them together). Of course, we do not live in a perfect world.

But the parent who says, "I'm gay," is telling his or her child that he or she has no intention of providing a parent of both sexes for that child. And a homosexual who "marries" someone of the same sex is declaring that this deprivation is to be permanent—and with the blessing of the state. . . .

More Children Would Grow Up Fatherless

This harm is closely related to the previous one, but worth noting separately. As more children, grow up without a married mother and father, they will be deprived of the tangible and intangible benefits and security that come from that family structure. However, most of those who live with only one biological parent will live with their mothers. In the general population, 79% of single-parent households are headed by the mother, compared to only 10% which are headed by the father. Among homosexual couples, as identified in the 2000 census, 34% of lesbian couples have children living at home, while only 22% of male couples were raising children. The encouragement of homosexual relationships that is intrinsic in the legalization of same-sex "marriage" would thus result in an increase in the number of children who suffer a specific set of negative consequences that are clearly associated with fatherlessness.

Homosexual activists say that having both a mother and a father simply does not matter—it is having two loving parents that counts. But social science research simply does not support this claim. Dr. Kyle Pruett of Yale Medical School, for example, has demonstrated in his book *Fatherneed* that fathers contribute to parenting in ways that mothers do not. Pruett declares, "From deep within their biological and psychological being, children need to connect to fathers . . . to live life whole." . . .

Extending the benefits and status of "marriage" to couples who are intrinsically incapable of natural procreation would dramatically change the social meaning of the institution.

Birth Rates Would Fall

One of the most fundamental tasks of any society is to reproduce itself. That is why virtually every human society up until the present day has given a privileged social status to male-female sexual relationships—the only type capable of resulting in natural procreation. This privileged social status is what we call "marriage."

Extending the benefits and status of "marriage" to couples who are intrinsically incapable of natural procreation (i.e., two men or two women) would dramatically change the social meaning of the institution. It would become impossible to argue that "marriage" is about encouraging the formation of life-long, potentially procreative (i.e., opposite-sex) relationships. The likely long-term result would be that fewer such relationships would be formed, fewer such couples would choose to procreate, and fewer babies would be born. . . .

Demands for Legalization of Polygamy Would Grow

If the natural sexual complementarity of male and female and the theoretical procreative capacity of an opposite-sex union are to be discarded as principles central to the definition of marriage, then what is left? According to the arguments of the homosexual "marriage" advocates, only love and companionship are truly necessary elements of marriage.

But if that is the case, then why should *other* relationships that provide love, companionship, and a lifelong commitment not *also* be recognized as "marriages"—including relationships between adults and children, or between blood relatives, or between three or more adults? And if it violates the equal protection of the laws to deny homosexuals their first choice of marital partner, why would it not do the same to deny pedophiles, polygamists, or the incestuous the right to marry the person (or persons) of their choice?

Of these, the road to polygamy seems the best-paved—and it is the most difficult for homosexual "marriage" advocates to deny. If, as they claim, it is arbitrary and unjust to limit the *gender* of one's marital partner, it is hard to explain why it would not be equally arbitrary and unjust to limit the *number* of marital partners.

There are also two other reasons why same-sex "marriage" advocates have trouble refuting warnings of a slippery slope toward polygamy. The first is that there is far more precedent cross-culturally for polygamy as an accepted marital structure than there is for homosexual "marriage." The second is that there is a genuine movement for polygamy or "polyamory" in some circles. . . .

Make no mistake about it—if same-sex "marriage" is not stopped now, we will have the exact same debate about "plural" marriages only one generation from now.

3

Same-Sex Marriage Is Harmful to Children

Trayce Hansen

Trayce Hansen is a licensed psychologist with a clinical and forensic practice and an interest in the areas of marriage, parenting, male/female differences, and homosexuality.

Supporters of same-sex marriage think that children really just need love, but this is not the case. Research shows that the ideal family structure for children is to be raised by both a mother and a father. Only this traditional type of family gives children the chance to relate to both a same-sex parent and a parent of the opposite sex. Although the research on same-sex parenting is very limited, some of it suggests that children raised in same-sex households will be more likely to be sexually confused and to experiment with sex. Also if same-sex marriage is allowed, it opens the door for other types of non-traditional marriage, such as polygamous relationships. Homosexual couples clearly can be just as loving to children as heterosexual couples, but love is not enough.

As mental health professionals, it's our ethical and moral obligation to support policies that are in the best interest of those we serve, particularly those who are most vulnerable—namely, children. Same-sex marriage may be in the best interest of adult homosexuals who yearn for social and legal recognition of their unions, but it's not in the best interest of children.

A Two-Parent, Mother-Father Family Is Ideal

Proponents of same-sex marriage believe love is all children really need. Based on that supposition, they conclude it's just as good for children to be raised by loving parents of the same sex, as by loving parents of the opposite sex. But that basic assumption—and all that flows from it—is naively simplistic and denies the complex nature and core needs of human beings.

Fathers reduce behavioral problems in boys and psychological problems in girls.

According to decades of research, the ideal family structure for children is a two-parent, mother-father family. That research consistently shows that children raised in such families are more likely to thrive—psychologically, mentally, and physically—than children reared in any other kind of family configuration.

Extensive research also reveals that not only mothers, but also fathers, are critical to the healthy development of children. Swedish researchers reviewed the best longitudinal studies from around the world that assessed the effects of fathers on children's development. Their review spanned 20 years of studies and included over 22,000 children, and found that fathers reduce behavioral problems in boys and psychological problems in girls, enhance cognitive development, and decrease delinquency.

It's clear that children benefit from having both a male and female parent. Recent medical research confirms genetically determined differences between men and women and those fundamental differences help explain why mothers and fathers bring unique characteristics to parenting that can't be replicated by the other sex. Mothers and fathers simply aren't interchangeable. Two women can both be good mothers, but neither can be a good father. One-sex parenting, whether by a single parent or a homosexual couple, deprives children of the full range of parenting offered by dual-sex couples.

Only mother-father families afford children the opportunity to develop relationships with a parent of the same, as well as the opposite sex. Relationships with both sexes early in life make it easier and more comfortable for a child to relate to both sexes later in life. Overall, having a relationship with both a male and female parent increases the likelihood that a child will have successful social and romantic relationships during his or her life.

Problems with Same-Sex Parented Families

Moreover, existing research on children reared by homosexuals is not only scientifically flawed and extremely limited but some of it actually indicates that those children are at increased risk for a variety of negative outcomes. Other studies find that homosexually parented children are more likely to experiment sexually, experience sexual confusion, and engage in homosexual and bisexual behavior themselves. And for those children who later engage in non-heterosexual behavior, extensive research reveals they are more likely to suffer from psychiatric disorders, abuse alcohol and drugs, attempt suicide, experience domestic violence and sexual assault, and are at increased risk for chronic diseases, AIDS, and shortened life spans.

Same-sex marriage no doubt will increase sexual confusion and sexual experimentation by young people.

It shouldn't be surprising that studies find children reared by homosexuals are more likely to engage in homosexual behavior themselves since extensive worldwide research reveals homosexuality is primarily environmentally induced. Specifically, social and/or family factors, as well as permissive environments which affirm homosexuality, play major environmental roles in the development of homosexual behavior. There's no question that human sexuality is fluid and pliant. Consider ancient Greece and Rome—among many early civilizations—where male homosexuality and bisexuality were nearly ubiquitous. That was not so because most of those men were born with a "gay gene," rather because sexuality is malleable and socially influenced.

Same-sex marriage no doubt will increase sexual confusion and sexual experimentation by young people, the implicit and explicit message of same-sex marriage is that all choices are equally acceptable and desirable. So even children from traditional homes—influenced by the all-sexual-options-are-equal message—will grow up thinking it doesn't matter whom one relates to sexually or marries. Holding such a belief will lead some—if not many—young people to consider sexual and marital arrangements they never would have contemplated previously.

It also must be expected that if society permits same-sex marriage, it also will have to allow other types of non-traditional marriage. The legal logic is simple: If prohibiting same-sex marriage is discriminatory, then disallowing polygamous marriage, polyamorous marriage, or any other marital grouping also will be deemed discriminatory. In fact, such legal maneuverings have already begun. The emotional and psychological ramifications of these assorted arrangements on the developing psyches and sexuality of children would be disastrous.

Fighting for the Needs of Children

To date, very little research exists that assesses long-term outcomes for homosexually parented children. According to Charlotte Patterson, a self-proclaimed, pro-same-sex-marriage researcher, there are only two longitudinal studies of children raised by lesbians. And no long-term studies of children raised by homosexual men. A professional organization dedicated to the welfare of its patients cannot and should not support drastic change in social policy based on just two, small and non-representative longitudinal studies.

Certainly homosexual couples can be just as loving toward children as heterosexual couples, but children need more than love. They require the distinctive qualities and complementary natures of a male and female parent. The accumulated wisdom of over 5,000 years concludes that the ideal marital and parental configuration is composed of one man and one woman. This time-tested wisdom is now supported by the most advanced, scientifically sound research available.

Importantly, and to their credit, many self-proclaimed pro-same-sex-marriage researchers acknowledge that there is as of yet no definitive evidence as to the impact of homosexual parenting on children. Regardless, some of those advocates support same-sex marriage because they believe it offers a natural laboratory in which to assess the long-term impact on children. That position is unconscionable and indefensible.

Same-sex marriage isn't in the best interest of children. While we may empathize with those homosexuals who long to be married and parent children, we mustn't allow our compassion for them to trump our compassion for children. In a contest between the desires of some homosexuals and the needs of all children, we cannot allow the children to lose.

4

Gay Marriage Is Not Harmful to Children

Brian Mustanski

Brian Mustanski is an assistant professor at the Institute for Juvenile Research at the University of Illinois at Chicago, and is the founding director of the IMPACT LGBT Health and Development Program, which conducts research on lesbian, gay, bisexual, and transgender health and development.

Advocates of gay marriage claim that children do fine when raised by gay parents and that marriage provides many psychological benefits. The research supports these positions. For example, studies show that children raised in homes with gay or lesbian parents develop as well as those in heterosexual marriages, on every level—emotional, cognitive, social, and sexual. Those who claim that kids do better with both a mom and a dad are often basing their arguments on research comparing two-parent heterosexual households with single parent homes. In addition, marriage confers a number of health and psychological benefits—such as having a shoulder to lean on, more income, and legal protections—and not providing these benefits leads to higher stress. In light of these findings, and since gay marriage doesn't hurt anyone, it should be allowed.

Between the popular vote to take away the marriage rights of same sex couples in California, passing of same-sex marriage bans in several states, and President-elect Barack

Obama including full civil unions for LGBT [lesbian, gay, bisexual, and transgender] couples as part of his civil rights platform, there has been a lot of recent attention on same sex relationships. Opponents of marriage rights for same sex couples generally argue that it redefines marriage away from its current and "traditional" form and that children are best raised by two opposite sex parents. Advocates for allowing same sex couples the right to marry argue that marriage confers over a thousand rights that they are currently denied, like the ability to inherit property, visit a sick partner in the hospital, and provide citizenship for non-citizen spouses.... Advocates also argue that children do just as well when raised by same-sex parents and that marriage provides a number of psychological and health benefits that they are currently denied.

Children who grow up with 1 or 2 gay and/or lesbian parents fare as well ... as do children whose parents are heterosexual.

I'm not a historian, but a quick read of the history of marriage makes it clear that it has evolved and changed throughout history and that the current version is a relatively recent phenomenon. That our current version of marriage is not "traditional" invalidates that argument against expanding it to include same sex couples, in my opinion. This leaves the real merits of the debate to center on positive and negative effects of marriage on same sex couples and their children. Fortunately, social scientists have been studying same sex couples and their children and their research provides much relevant information.

Well-Being of Children

One of the most widely cited arguments against allowing same sex couples marriages rights is that it could harm children raised in the context of these relationships. Upon examination of the social science research in this area it is clear that the evidence does not support this argument. According to a report by the American Academy of Pediatrics, "A growing body of scientific literature demonstrates that children who grow up with 1 or 2 gay and/or lesbian parents fare as well in emotional, cognitive, social, and sexual functioning as do children whose parents are heterosexual. Children's optimal development seems to be influenced more by the nature of the relationships and interactions within the family unit than by the particular structural form it takes." Since that report was published in 2002, a number of additional studies have been published showing that children with same sex parents do at least as well on the outcomes studied as children as opposite sex parents. This is why the other major psychological and health organizations have made resolutions supporting same sex marriage and parenting.

Last year I did a television news interview about the issue of same sex couples raising children. During the segment they showed a clip of me describing the social science evidence, and then they showed a clip of a religious figure saying that research shows kids are better off with a "mom and a dad." I was disappointed that they showed this clip because I had explained to the reporters that this issue often gets confused by making inappropriate comparisons. In the case of the religious figure, he was referring to research showing that children raised with a mom and a dad look better on some outcomes than children raised by a single parent. Most of these differences are explained by the socioeconomic strain of being a single parent. But comparing children raised by a mother and a father to children raised by a single parent tells us nothing about how well children will do when they are raised by two same sex parents. The appropriate research approach would be to compare children raised by same or opposite sex parents. And these kinds of comparisons make it clear that children raised by same sex parents do just fine. Making other comparisons is, at best misguided, and at worst purposefully disingenuous.

Benefits of Marriage

In addition to the legal rights that come with marriage, there are a number of well known psychological and health benefits of being married. It should come to no surprise that having a shoulder to lean on during difficult times, a partner contributing income and effort to sustaining the household, legal protections of your relationship, and a person to help multiply the joys of life has many health benefits. More recently, research has shown that making it more difficult for some people to reap these benefits imposes health risks. The January 2009 issue of the *Journal of Counseling Psychology* has several articles reporting novel research on this topic. According to the press release for the issue, "Amendments that restrict civil marriage rights of same-sex couples—such as Proposition 8 that recently passed in California—have led to higher levels of stress and anxiety among lesbian, gay, bisexual and transgender adults, as well as among their families of origin, according to several new studies to be published by the American Psychological Association." The release reports results from an online study of 1,552 lesbian, gay and bisexual adults from all 50 states and the District of Columbia. According to the researchers, led by Dr. Sharon Scales Rostosky, at the University of Kentucky, "The results of this study demonstrate that living in a state that has just passed a marriage amendment is associated with higher levels of psychological stress for lesbian, gay and bisexual citizens," Rostosky said. "And this stress is not due to other pre-existing conditions or factors; it is a direct result of the negative images and messages associated with the ballot campaign and the passage of the amendment."

The results of this and other studies suggest that denying same sex couples marriage rights not only prevents them from reaping the psychological and health benefits of marriage, but the process of codifying the elimination of these rights has negative psychological impacts on LGBT people.

Given the scientific evidence of the positive effects of same sex marriage on couples, the lack of negative effects on children reared in the context of these relationships, and the harm caused by preventing or eliminating marriage equality it doesn't seem that there is a solid foundation to stand on when arguing against allowing same sex couples to wed. From my perspective, it comes down to common sense. If it helps some people and it doesn't hurt anyone, why not let in happen. I think the comedian Wanda Sykes put it best, "It's real simple. If you don't believe in same-sex marriage, don't marry someone of the same sex." In other words, why not allow gay marriage?

5

Gay Marriage Could Infringe on Religious Liberties

Bobby Ross Jr.

Bobby Ross Jr. is a reporter and editor who has written for both secular and religious media. He currently is managing editor of The Christian Chronicle, *an international newspaper for Churches of Christ.*

The New York same sex marriage legislation has caused some conservatives to conclude that the battle against gay marriage should shift to protecting religious freedom. This is because more and more states are likely to pass gay marriage bills, and unless these bills contain religious liberty protections, churches and religious organizations may face challenges when upholding their convictions. For example, faith-based organizations might be challenged on their right to refuse adoption services to same-sex couples. The New York law does protect churches and religious organizations from having to perform same-sex marriages or accept gay couples into their memberships. For now, however, the fight continues to focus on opposing any form of gay marriage legislation.

W as the shot heard 'round the evangelical world fired June 24 [2011] in New York?

The passage of a same-sex marriage law by that state's Republican-controlled Senate sent a clear message, a leading religious liberty expert says.

That message: Religious conservatives who advocate traditional marriage must shift their focus to fighting for religious freedom.

"It's just a matter of time before it's possible to enact these bills in more and more states," said Douglas Laycock, a law professor at the University of Virginia. "The greater the support, the less leverage anyone trying to get a religious liberty provision [will have]. The time to get protection for religious liberty in these bills is now, while they're still difficult for the supporters to enact."

Protecting Faith-Based Institutions

Stanley Carlson-Thies, president of the Institutional Religious Freedom Alliance, isn't ready to advocate such a drastic detour—at least not yet.

But as more states pass civil-union and same-sex marriage laws, he acknowledges a need for gay-marriage opponents to press for language in such laws that protects faith-based organizations.

Lawmakers won the religious liberty exemptions at the expense of sticking with their moral convictions on traditional marriage.

"The religious-freedom consequence of these changes is increasingly recognized and increasingly seen as something that needs to have a focus of its own," he said.

In New York, in fact, "more expansive protections for religious organizations" helped win support from four Republicans who voted with the Democratic minority and put the bill over the top, *The New York Times* reported. Carlson-Thies complained, however, that lawmakers won the religious liberty exemptions at the expense of sticking with their moral convictions on traditional marriage.

Laycock said the New York law clearly protects churches and religious organizations from having to perform same-sex marriage ceremonies or welcome gay couples into their memberships.

But the language is "so badly drafted" that it's difficult to assess what the impact might be, for example, on a faith-based organization that wants to refuse to provide adoption services to a same-sex couple, he said.

Now, the question seems to be: Can faith-based agencies with conscientious objections refuse to place children with gay and unmarried couples?

Just a few years ago, a key question in the public square was: Would gay and unmarried couples be allowed to adopt children or serve as foster parents?

Now, the question seems to be: Can faith-based agencies with conscientious objections refuse to place children with gay and unmarried couples?

"It's a question of: Can religious organizations continue to operate for the public good in a way that's consistent with their convictions?" said Jedd Medefind, president of the Christian Alliance for Orphans.

In June, before the New York vote, Carlson-Thies praised the "robust language" in a Rhode-Island civil-union bill that he said offered sufficient protections for religious organizations with sincerely held religious convictions against civil unions.

But that same month in Illinois, which began recognizing civil unions June 1, a Catholic Charities organization in Rockford halted its state-funded foster care and adoption services rather than face potential liability for failing to place children with parents in civil unions. Meanwhile, three Roman Catholic dioceses—Springfield, Peoria, and Joliet—filed a lawsuit seeking confirmation that they're acting within existing law by offering adoption and foster-care services only to married couples and non-cohabiting single individuals.

Similar battles have occurred in the District of Columbia, Virginia, and Massachusetts. Religious-freedom questions will be on statewide ballots in North Dakota and Missouri in 2012.

Ramifications Beyond Adoption

The ramifications extend far beyond adoption, Carlson-Thies said, touching on, for example, a Christian college's right to hire employees who abide by its sexual standards, or a faith-based drug treatment facility's ability to advertise a mentor position for a husband and wife.

Such organizations should not let states "run roughshod" over their religious freedom, he said: "We ought to stand on our constitutional rights and try to get them into the law, and if they're not gotten into the law, then stand up in other ways."

Laycock is part of a small group of law professors who have been lobbying state legislatures across the nation for religious-liberty provisions in such measures.

Despite his contention that religious conservatives "absolutely" need to change strategy, Laycock stops short of predicting that will happen.

"My sense," he said, "is still that both sides are just dug in and want to completely squash the other side, so the religious conservatives are opposed to any form of same-sex marriage and the gay-rights side are opposed to any form of religious-liberty protection."

6

Gay Marriage Is a Human Rights Issue

Marianne Mollmann

Marianne Mollmann is the advocacy director of the Women's Rights Division, a project of Human Rights Watch, a nongovernmental organization based in New York and dedicated to protecting human rights around the world.

Gay marriage is really a matter of respect and human rights. Across the world, gays are subjected to violence simply because they are gay, and the United Nations Human Rights Council has recently condemned this violence. But it is not just violence that violates the human rights of gays; a similar rights violation takes place whenever gays are treated as different and less than heterosexuals, such as when they are denied the right to marry. Marriage by itself does not guarantee good family relationships, but because family leave and many other benefits are available only to married couples, children suffer if their gay parents are not permitted to marry.

Earlier this year, a student in a human rights seminar I was teaching declared her conviction that gay parents damage their children by virtue of being gay. I explained as gently as I could why this is a discriminatory notion, incompatible with human rights standards, and moved on. My student sat as if stunned for two minutes, then gathered her books and left the class.

She later confronted me outside the classroom, and I was astonished to see just how fervently she insisted that her opinion was both based on science and respectful of rights. Neither is true. As New York State joins the ranks of countries and other jurisdictions recognizing same-sex marriage, it's worth reflecting on rights and respect.

Treating Gays As Lesser People

The fact is that thousands of human beings are subjected to violence across the globe simply because they are suspected of being gay. In Brazil alone, over 2,500 men were murdered between 1997 and 2007, ostensibly for being gay. In the United States, the It Gets Better Project has highlighted the sustained violence and bullying young people suffer just because they aren't straight. This month, the United Nations Human Rights Council for the first time condemned violence and other human rights violations based on a person's sexual orientation or identity.

For too many people it is only a short leap from seeing homosexuality as offensive to justifying physical harm.

Of course, those who oppose same-sex marriage in New York State and elsewhere are not saying they support violence against LGBTQ [lesbian, gay, bisexual, transgender, and queer] people. Nevertheless, the same basic proposition lies at the root of both: the notion that you are somehow a different—lesser—type of human being if you are not, or are not seen to be, straight, and that society is justified in rejecting you.

For too many people it is only a short leap from seeing homosexuality as offensive to justifying physical harm. In this way, for example, the ban on inter-racial marriage in this country coexisted with societal acceptance of violence against people of color. Many times, inter-racial couples suffered violence precisely because they dared to break the ban.

Gay Marriage and Children

But perhaps the deepest-held notion is the one that was expressed so vehemently by my student: that all children brought up by LGBTQ persons are psychologically damaged. Fortunately, it is increasingly recognized that it is not exposure to diversity but rather to bigotry and prejudice that is damaging to kids. In 2008, the European Court on Human Rights held that France was not allowed to deny the adoption application of a woman just because she was a lesbian. And in February, the High Court in the United Kingdom barred a couple from becoming foster parents because their anti-gay views were held to be potentially harmful to the children who would be in their care.

In fact, research shows that children with gay parents are just as likely to be well-adjusted as children with straight parents, and that the key to childhood adjustment is good relationships between parents and children and between the parents themselves. Marriage, of course, does not guarantee good relationships. But where family leave and other benefits depend on marital status, children are disadvantaged if their parents are not allowed to marry. The vote in Albany [New York] this week is significant because it is another step toward guaranteeing children and adults the rights and respect they are entitled to.

7

Gay Marriage Is Protected by the US Constitution

David Boies

David Boies is an attorney and chairman of the New York law firm of Boies, Schiller, and Flexner.

Gay marriage is not a liberal or conservative issue, but an issue of enforcing the US Constitution's guarantee of equal protection and due process to all Americans. Just like skin color, sexual orientation is an immutable characteristic, so the gay minority must be protected from discrimination just as racial minorities are protected. Accordingly, the constitutional right to marry cannot be subject to a majority vote. The Constitution does guarantee freedom of religion for those who see homosexuality as inconsistent with their religion, but it also states that religious beliefs cannot be the basis for anti-gay rights legislation. It is time to end centuries of discrimination against gays and lesbians by upholding the Constitution's equal protection guarantees and eliminating state laws against gay marriage.

When I got married in California in 1959 there were almost 20 states where marriage was limited to two people of different sexes and the same race. Eight years later the Supreme Court unanimously declared state bans on interracial marriage unconstitutional.

Recently, [attorney] Ted Olson and I brought a lawsuit asking the courts to now declare unconstitutional California's

Proposition 8 limitation of marriage to people of the opposite sex. We acted together because of our mutual commitment to the importance of this cause, and to emphasize that this is not a Republican or Democratic issue, not a liberal or conservative issue, but an issue of enforcing our Constitution's guarantee of equal protection and due process to all citizens.

A Constitutional Right to Marry

The [US] Supreme Court has repeatedly held that the right to marry the person you love is so fundamental that states cannot abridge it. In 1978 the Court (8 to 1, *Zablocki v. Redhail*) overturned as unconstitutional a Wisconsin law preventing child-support scofflaws [people who fail to pay court-ordered support for their children] from getting married. The Court emphasized, "decisions of this Court confirm that the right to marry is of fundamental importance for all individuals." In 1987 the Supreme Court unanimously struck down as unconstitutional a Missouri law preventing imprisoned felons from marrying.

Countries as Catholic as Spain, as different as Sweden and South Africa, and as near as Canada have embraced gay and lesbian marriage without any noticeable effect.

There were legitimate state policies that supported the Wisconsin and Missouri restrictions held unconstitutional. By contrast, there is no legitimate state policy underlying Proposition 8. The occasional suggestion that marriages between people of different sexes may somehow be threatened by marriages of people of the same sex does not withstand discussion. It is difficult to the point of impossibility to envision two love-struck heterosexuals contemplating marriage to decide against it because gays and lesbians also have the right to marry; it is equally hard to envision a couple whose marriage is troubled basing the decision of whether to divorce on whether their gay neighbors are married or living in a domestic partnership. And even if depriving lesbians of the right to marry each other could force them into marrying someone they do not love but who happens to be of the opposite sex, it is impossible to see how that could be thought to be as likely to lead to a stable, loving relationship as a marriage to the person they do love.

Moreover, there is no longer any credible contention that depriving gays and lesbians of basic rights will cause them to change their sexual orientation. Even if there was, the attempt would be constitutionally defective. But, in fact, the sexual orientation of gays and lesbians is as much a God-given characteristic as the color of their skin or the sexual orientation of their straight brothers and sisters. It is also a condition that, like race, has historically been subject to abusive and often violent discrimination. It is precisely where a minority's basic human rights are abridged that our Constitution's promise of due process and equal protection is most vital.

Ending Oppression of Gays and Lesbians

Countries as Catholic as Spain, as different as Sweden and South Africa, and as near as Canada have embraced gay and lesbian marriage without any noticeable effect—except the increase in human happiness and social stability that comes from permitting people to marry for love. Several states—including Connecticut, Iowa, Maine, Massachusetts, New Hampshire and Vermont—have individually repealed their bans on same-sex marriage as inconsistent with a decent respect for human rights and a rational view of the communal value of marriage for all individuals. But basic constitutional rights cannot depend on the willingness of the electorate in any given state to end discrimination. If we were prepared to consign minority rights to a majority vote, there would be no need for a constitution.

The ban on same-sex marriages written into the California Constitution by a 52% vote in favor of Proposition 8 is the residue of centuries of figurative and literal gay-bashing. California allows same-sex domestic partnerships that, as interpreted by the California Supreme Court, provide virtually all of the economic rights of marriage. So the ban on permitting gay and lesbian couples to actually marry is simply an attempt by the state to stigmatize a segment of its population that commits no offense other than falling in love with a disapproved partner, and asks no more of the state than to be treated equally with all other citizens. In 2003 the United States Supreme Court in *Lawrence v. Texas* held that states could not constitutionally outlaw consensual homosexual activity. As Justice Anthony Kennedy elegantly wrote rejecting the notion that a history of discrimination might trump constitutional rights, "Times can blind us to certain truths and later generations can see that laws once thought necessary and proper in fact serve only to oppress. As the Constitution endures, persons in every generation can invoke its principles in their own search for greater freedom."

There are those who sincerely believe that homosexuality is inconsistent with their religion—and the First Amendment guarantees their freedom of belief. However, the same First Amendment, as well as the Due Process and Equal Protection clauses, preclude the enshrinement of their religious-based disapproval in state law.

Gays and lesbians are our brothers and sisters, our teachers and doctors, our friends and neighbors, our parents and children. It is time, indeed past time, that we accord them the basic human right to marry the person they love. It is time, indeed past time, that our Constitution fulfill its promise of equal protection and due process for all citizens by now eliminating the last remnant of centuries of misguided state discrimination against gays and lesbians.

The argument in favor of Proposition 8 ultimately comes down to no more than the tautological assertion that a marriage is between a man and a woman. But a slogan is not a substitute for constitutional analysis. Law is about justice, not bumper stickers.

8

There Are Several Constitutional Hurdles to Gay Marriage

Ron Trowbridge

Ron Trowbridge was appointed chief of staff to Chief Justice Warren Burger and the Commission on the Bicentennial of the US Constitution.

Supporters of gay marriage argue that it is a legal right, but this is based on one interpretation of the 14th Amendment of the US Constitution. According to several Supreme Court cases, the equal protection clause of the 14th Amendment can be interpreted in numerous ways. Although the 14th Amendment is cited as a means to defend and protect gay marriage, there is "no settled, absolute standard of what the clause 'equal protection of the laws' means." Since gay marriage may not be a natural right protected by the US Constitution, appellate courts may rule that states should decide the issue of gay marriage.

U. S. District Court Judge Vaughn Walker's recent reversal of the ban on gay marriage in California could itself in appellate courts be reversed. The following are six possible areas of constitutional dispute.

One, some argue that the Equal Protection Clause of the 14th Amendment protects gay marriage. But there is no settled, absolute standard of what the clause "equal protection of the laws" means. Some use the clause to defend affirmative action, insisting such action is first necessary for minorities to be brought up the starting line to enter the race with equality.

If the precedent of secular private contracts is widely broadened, such will protect private contracts for polygamy, adultery, pornography and prostitution.

Others, directly to the contrary, argue that affirmative action violates the equal protection clause because it sanctions discriminatory acts in favor of certain groups over other groups. Hence, because Judge X believes that the 14th Amendment protects gay marriage does not mean that Judge Y does.

Two, one of the arguments in Walker's court in defense of gay marriage is that it is, as counsel David Boies asserted, a "private contract"—such as we see enumerated in Article I, Section 8 of the Constitution, which declares that no law can impair the "obligation of contracts." But if a private contract between two consenting adults is legal, by what legal logic can a private marriage contract between, say, a consenting man and two consenting women not be constitutionally protected?

If the precedent of secular private contracts is widely broadened, such will protect private contracts for polygamy, adultery, pornography and prostitution.

Constitutional vs. Fundamental Rights

Three, what makes a right constitutional or fundamental? A fundamental right, according to the standard in *Washington v. Glucksberg* (1997), is one that is "deeply rooted in this nation's history and traditions" and "implicit in the concept of ordered liberty." While homosexuality is ancient, gay marriage itself is not deeply rooted in this nation's history and traditions.

Four, a fundamental right requires a "rational basis." The rational basis for a marriage between a man and a woman is to create the perpetuation of life on Earth. Gay couples alone cannot create life. Gay marriage therefore is not equal to heterosexual marriage and therefore might not be protected by the Equal Protection Clause.

Five, all judges are governed to some degree by a judicial philosophy. They do not come to the bench with blank minds. Justice Antonin Scalia's judicial philosophy is different from Justice Ruth Bader Ginsburg's. Scalia is generally conservative; Ginsburg, generally liberal. Judge Walker has a judicial philosophy, too, but it could be countered by different philosophies in appellate courts.

Six, there is a question of jurisdiction. The equal protection clause of the 14th Amendment is cited as protecting gay marriage. But there is also a 10th Amendment that declares that "powers not delegated to the United States by the Constitution . . . are reserved to the states." Appellate courts could rule that jurisdiction of gay marriage rests with the states.

My own personal views on gay marriage are irrelevant, but I do assert that the constitutionality of gay marriage is now subject to large hurdles. Due process through appellate courts could take two to four years.

9

The Defense of Marriage Act Should Be Defended in the Courts

Hans von Spakovsky

Hans von Spakovsky is a senior legal fellow at the Center for Legal and Judicial Studies, where he manages the Civil Justice Reform Initiative. The Center is a project of the Heritage Foundation, a conservative think tank.

President Barack Obama's decision not to defend the Defense of Marriage Act (DOMA) is serious because it is well established that the Justice Department should defend a federal statute unless no reasonable argument can be made in its defense. The Executive branch has applied this principle on numerous occasions and vigorously defended statutes even when it had strong policy reservations about doing so. However, President Obama is violating that tradition as well as his constitutional duty by clearly seeking to undermine DOMA. Because of this Executive branch decision, the courts should permit statements by members of Congress or others who can competently argue for upholding DOMA.

Today [February 23, 2011], President Barack Obama concluded, and Attorney General Eric Holder announced, that the administration will not defend the Defense of Marriage Act (DOMA). DOMA defines marriage as between a man and a woman for the purposes of federal law, and clari-

Hans von Spakovsky, "Obama Drops Pretense, Administration Will Not Defend DOMA," *The Foundry*, February 23, 2011. Copyright © 2011 by The Heritage Foundation. All rights reserved. Reproduced by permission.

fies that no state has to recognize a homosexual marriage from another state. The President's announcement is refreshing in its honesty, at least insofar as it drops the farce that the administration has been offering anything even remotely approaching a vigorous (and professional) defense of the federal statute.

On this count, even supporters of gay marriage have acknowledged that the Justice Department's non-defense of DOMA to date has bordered on creating collusive litigation, and concluded that the "DOJ's faint-hearted advocacy is no way to run a legal system." So, notwithstanding the President's desire to undermine DOMA, his non-enforcement may actually bolster its prospect in the courts: by getting out of the way, the Justice Department will make way for competent and vigorous legal defense of the statute.

There are reasonable legal arguments to be made in defense of DOMA.

A Serious Decision Based on Policy

But the President's decision is nonetheless a serious one. While the President has a duty to interpret the Constitution through his decisions to enforce statutes, it is the well-established policy of the Justice Department to defend a federal statute unless no reasonable argument may be made in its defense, or unless the statute would infringe on some core presidential constitutional authority (that is, the President doesn't need to vigorously defend a federal statute that he believes infringes on his Article II power). Applying this policy, the Executive Branch has traditionally defended federal statutes vigorously, even in cases where it had strong constitutional doubts, and where it had strong policy reservations.

For example, in his signing statement for the Bipartisan Campaign Reform Act, President Bush expressed his view that certain provisions of the act were likely unconstitutional. Yet, the President and his Justice Department, through Solicitor General Ted Olson, vigorously defended the entire bill, including those constitutionally deficient provisions. Olson succeeded in his defense, although he successfully attacked provisions of the same bill as unconstitutional after he left the Justice Department.

There are reasonable legal arguments to be made in defense of DOMA. The Justice Department's failure to make them to date, and the President's abandonment of the case, appear to be judgments made not based on a determination of the availability of reasonable legal arguments, but based upon the policy preferences of the President. That has never been the standard used by the Justice Department or any prior administration.

The President is now required by federal law (28 U.S.C. § 530D) to file a report to Congress within 30 days explaining the decision not to defend the law, "including a complete and detailed statement of the reasons for the policy or determination. . . ." The courts of appeals will need to appoint counsel to defend the law.

Members of Congress, consistent with the law of standing, should seek to intervene in the case or file amicus briefs [written statements] to assure that DOMA gets the vigorous defense that should be afforded to all federal statutes for which reasonable legal arguments may be offered—and which the President is refusing to provide. Furthermore, the court should give special consideration to such intervening or amicus briefs as statements of the federal government in support of a statute, given the complete failure of the President to carry out his constitutional duty to "take care that the laws be faithfully executed."

10

The Defense of Marriage Act Should Not Be Defended in the Courts

Dahlia Lithwick

Dahlia Lithwick is a contributing editor at Newsweek *magazine and senior editor at* Slate, *an online magazine of politics, news, and culture.*

The federal government is obligated to enforce and defend the nation's laws whether the president agrees with the laws or not. However, the Barack Obama administration is justified in its decision to no longer defend Section 3 of the Defense of Marriage Act (DOMA) in the courts, because it violates the equal protection clause of the US Constitution. As Attorney General Eric Holder has explained, the administration will continue to enforce DOMA but will not defend it, because the law cannot pass the type of heightened scrutiny required by the US Constitution. The law cannot be defended under this standard because the legislative record contains many anti-gay and stereotype-based statements—the kind of discrimination that the equal protection clause has historically prohibited. In the future, therefore, Congress will have to defend DOMA in the courts, and ultimately the constitutionality of DOMA may be decided by the US Supreme Court.

Dahlia Lithwick, "Indefensible: Why the Obama Administration Changed Its Mind About the Defense of Marriage Act," *Slate.com*, February 23, 2011. Copyright © 2011 by *Slate.com*. All rights reserved. Reproduced by permission.

The real surprise on Wednesday [February 23, 2011] wasn't that the [Barack] Obama administration decided it could no longer legally defend the federal Defense of Marriage Act [DOMA], which mandates that the federal government not recognize same-sex marriages and stipulates that states need not recognize same-sex marriages from other states. It's that it took so long to get here. Recall that presidential candidate Barack Obama pledged to repeal the law, which he had called "abhorrent," in 2007. What needed to be bridged over the past two years was the distance between the president's personal views and his duty to defend a congressional statute.

Refusing to Defend DOMA

That's why even as the Justice Department [DOJ] opted to defend the law at every legal turn, it did so claiming that "until Congress passes legislation repealing the law, the administration will continue to defend the statute when it is challenged in the justice system." As Walter Dellinger, acting solicitor general in the Clinton administration, has explained: "The government has an obligation to comply with the nation's laws, regardless of whether the president agrees with a particular statute. Doing otherwise would also set a precedent justifying similar nullifications by future administrations." The alternative, according to Dellinger, would be to have every president nullify the laws passed by his predecessors by simply declining to appeal adverse rulings.

Dellinger's proposed middle way—in the context of the October court rulings striking down the military's "Don't Ask, Don't Tell" policy—was to have the administration continue to defend the law formally in the courts while suggesting reasons the courts should strike the law down. This has happened before: The Clinton administration both enforced and argued against a discriminatory HIV policy in the military in 1996, and the law was repealed. That's precisely what the administration opted to do with DOMA on Wednesday.

Attorney General Eric Holder's letter to Congress said the Obama administration would no longer defend Section 3—and only Section 3—of DOMA in New York and Connecticut because it violates the equal-protection clause of the Fifth Amendment, as applied to same-sex couples. Last July, a federal judge in Massachusetts declared DOMA unconstitutional, because it denied federal benefits to legally married same-sex couples in the state. The Obama administration appealed that decision in January, much to the dismay of gay-marriage supporters, who argued that fighting to uphold a discriminatory law in the courts was proof of the administration's ongoing hostility to gay rights. References in government briefs to "uncles marrying nieces" weren't helping.

The administration will continue to enforce DOMA— but it won't defend it.

Section 3 provides that "in determining the meaning of any Act of Congress, or of any ruling, regulation, or interpretation of the various administrative bureaus and agencies of the United States, the word 'marriage' means only a legal union between one man and one woman as husband and wife, and the word 'spouse' refers only to a person of the opposite sex who is a husband or a wife." From now on, explained Holder, the administration will continue to enforce DOMA—but it won't defend it, because it doesn't pass the heightened standard of scrutiny it should receive in the courts.

As Adam Bonin lays it out here, bumping up the standard of review isn't mere legal semantics. In his letter, Holder explains that the administration "has defended Section 3 in jurisdictions where circuit courts have already held that classifications based on sexual orientation are subject to rational basis review, and it has advanced arguments to defend DOMA Section 3 under the binding standard that has applied in those cases." "Rational basis review" means that courts will uphold the law so long as it is rationally related to a legitimate government interest. It's the most deferential standard of review, and, Holder suggests, the administration could muster the arguments to defend it in the jurisdictions that applied that test. (Although Holder then goes on in his letter to pillory even the "rational" reasons often advanced to discriminate against gay marriage, including arguments about "'procreational responsibility' that the department has disavowed already in litigation as unreasonable, or claims regarding the immutability of sexual orientation that we do not believe can be reconciled with more recent social science understandings.")

Congress will have to defend DOMA, and Justice Department attorneys will now argue that heightened scrutiny should apply ... and eventually these cases will reach the Supreme Court.

The Winds of Change

What's really changed since last fall, according to Holder's reasoning, is that since November 2010, two new lawsuits were filed challenging Section 3 of DOMA in jurisdictions without any precedent indicating whether classifications based on sexual orientation would be subject to the lower "rational basis review" or something higher. Reflecting on the appropriate standard of review, the administration concluded that "the legislative record underlying DOMA's passage contains discussion and debate that undermines any defense under heightened scrutiny. The record contains numerous expressions reflecting moral disapproval of gays and lesbians and their intimate and family relationships—precisely the kind of stereotype-based thinking and animus the Equal Protection Clause is designed to guard against."

Translation: Members of Congress can continue to say what they please to justify passing a law. But we can no longer stand up and make these sorts of arguments in front of a judge.

Holder is careful to minimize the impact of what happens next. It's not as though the whole law will collapse under the weight of "heightened scrutiny" tomorrow. Going forward, Congress will have to defend DOMA, and Justice Department attorneys will now argue that heightened scrutiny should apply. Presumably, someone other than the Justice Department will step in to file briefs defending DOMA, and eventually these cases will reach the Supreme Court. But the DOJ will still play a role. "If asked by the district courts in the Second Circuit for the position of the United States in the event those courts determine that the applicable standard is rational basis," Holder writes, "the Department will state that . . . a reasonable argument for Section 3's constitutionality may be proffered under that permissive standard."

The real sea change here is that Obama can finally claim, as his attorney general did today, that the winds of change have shifted since 1996. "The Supreme Court has ruled that laws criminalizing homosexual conduct are unconstitutional," writes Holder today. "Congress has repealed the military's Don't Ask, Don't Tell policy. Several lower courts have ruled DOMA itself to be unconstitutional." Obama can now openly state that his views on gay marriage are "evolving" as Holder admits that "recent evolutions" in gay rights law have influenced this change.

The president seems to have finally acknowledged a truth played out at the Proposition 8 trial in California last summer: Virtually all of the arguments advanced to deny gay couples the right to marry are based on moral animus and junk science, rooted in discredited cases like *Bowers v. Hardwick* and in unfounded bias that is increasingly hard to defend in open court. As professor Suzanne Goldberg of Columbia

Law School put it today: "This is a spectacular and long-awaited acknowledgment by the federal government that there is no good reason for treating gay and nongay people differently, especially when it comes to recognizing the relationships of same-sex couples." The main consequence of today's decision is that the people who actually believe in *Bowers v. Hardwick*, moral animus, and junk science will get to defend it in court, if they can. The president no longer has to.

11

The Defense of Marriage Act Should Be Repealed

Rudy Molinet

Rudy Molinet is a real estate broker in Key West, Florida, and a community and human rights activist.

The 14th Amendment of the US Constitution clearly affords all US citizens equal protection under the law, and the Defense of Marriage Act (DOMA) unfairly denies gay and lesbian couples equal protection. President Barack Obama is right to not defend DOMA, and is showing political courage by standing up for the civil rights of gay and lesbian Americans. Just a few short decades ago, gays and lesbians were subjected to terrible violence and injustices, but now things are rapidly changing for the better. All Americans should unite to repeal DOMA to end attacks on the civil rights of gays and lesbians.

The Republican-controlled House of Representatives decided that it would start this year's [2011] congressional session by having members of congress read the Constitution. A very noble idea and one that I thought was a worthy exercise. Though you have to wonder if they actually listened to what was being read in those hallowed halls of American power—or did they just happen to skip over the 14th Amendment?

The 14th Amendment of the United States Constitution is very clear. All citizens of the United States are afforded equal protection of the laws. President [Barack] Obama, a constitutional lawyer, has actually read and listened to the Constitution and has directed the United States Justice Department to no longer defend the discriminatory so-called Defense of Marriage Act (DOMA). This is a groundbreaking moment for lesbian, gay, bisexual and transgender Americans and our quest for equality in this nation.

An Unfair and Unconstitutional Law

DOMA was passed by a Republican Congress and signed into law by a Democratic president [Bill Clinton] in 1996—a different era in this country's history toward acceptance of gay and lesbian citizens and our right to full and equal protection of the laws. This law unfairly—and now, according to President Obama—unconstitutionally, denies gay and lesbian married couples equal protection and recognition of their legally performed marriages in several U.S. states and multiple countries. The law is trumpeted by the same Republicans and tea partyers who proclaim states' rights and preach the virtues of limited federal powers.

So let me get this straight (pun intended), these folks don't want the federal government to assure that every American has the right to health care, but want the same federal government to tell me who I can love? Really?

A Historic Change

President Obama is becoming for gay and lesbian Americans what [Presidents] Harry Truman and Lyndon Johnson were to African-Americans. Truman and Johnson risked their political careers to do what they thought was right and the "American" thing to do. Truman integrated the military and Johnson signed dozens of historic civil rights laws that changed the character of a nation.

No longer would African-Americans have to drink from separate water fountains, nor be educated in inferior schools disguised by the mantra of "separate but equal." Never again would a black man be relegated to the back of the bus or a black woman prohibited from marrying a white man. Our nation is a better place because equality and fairness ruled the day.

President Obama, a product of his two predecessors' vision, will be remembered in history as a man who understood the importance of equality, and his life story is a living example of the power of equality in our nation.

We are at the dawn of a new age of equality for gays and lesbians that no one would have even dreamed of 30 years ago. The Stonewall Riots of 1969 launched the modern-day gay rights movement. For three days, gay men, women and drag queens fought for their lives and for our rights against constant harassment by the New York Police Department and raised awareness of the injustices suffered by gay and lesbian Americans.

Now is the time . . . to defeat the Defense of Marriage Act. This law is unconstitutional and an indecent and horrendous attack on the civil liberties of gays and lesbians.

We have the pleasure of knowing several gay octogenarians who lived through that era. Among them are [the author's spouse] Harry's Uncle Donald and his partner, Frank. Donald and Frank have been a couple for over 45 years. They came from an era that precluded most people from being openly gay. They share stories that today would seem incredible. When they were younger in New York and were at a bar, if they were even caught holding hands they would be subject to arrest. They could have never fathomed openly gay people on television or in Congress or in the halls of justice—and certainly not same-sex marriage in places like Iowa!

Yet same-sex marriage is now the law of the land in several states, civil unions are spreading through the land and courts are beginning to rule DOMA unconstitutional. It is just a matter of time. In the past two weeks, Hawaii and Illinois approved civil unions for gay couples, and Maryland is at the verge of approving same-sex marriage.

Now is the time for all good men and women of the United States to unite to defeat the Defense of Marriage Act. This law is unconstitutional and an indecent and horrendous attack on the civil liberties of gays and lesbians. After all, in a nation that "holds these truths to be self-evident that all men are created equal," can we really tolerate a law that relegates gay and lesbian families to the back of the bus? I don't think so!

12

The US Supreme Court Will Likely Rule in Favor of Gay Marriage

Mathew S. Urdan

Mathew S. Urdan contributes to the Inside Government blog, a non-partisan effort to examine how the US government works.

Ever since 2003, when the Massachusetts Supreme Court held that laws prohibiting gay marriage were unconstitutional, the topic of gay marriage has become a contentious public issue. However, this issue and the status of homosexual men and women in this country will no doubt remain fluid until the matter is decided by the US Supreme Court. A review of the Supreme Court's decisions suggests that the Court is concerned about the human dignity of gay citizens. The issue will be decided ultimately on an interpretation of the equal protection clause contained in the Fourteenth Amendment of the US Constitution. Although judicial decision-making can be a long process, it is likely that the Supreme Court will eventually rule that same-sex marriage is constitutional under the Fourteenth Amendment.

America is at a major crossroads and it is time to decide what we want for our society. Do we want to work together to solve our issues and contribute to the positive growth of our nation or do we want to live in a society of hate where the left and the right are always at odds, where bullying and scapegoating is accepted? Do we want to lead the world in the promotion of human rights and democracy, or do we want to be the bully imposing our will on sovereign nations for our own benefit, even if our actions conflict with our most cherished ideals?

In many ways, our response to gay marriage is a microcosm of these larger questions. Paradoxically, while we condemn nations like China for their human rights violations, we still embrace racist practices here at home and give hate a forum. The [Barack] Obama administration's decision to no longer support the Defense of Marriage Act (DOMA) is a step in the right direction to end one of our nation's last great frontiers of hate and denial of dignity and respect to a significant segment of our nation's citizens. It is probably the best decision of Obama's presidency to date, no matter what your politics and views regarding gay marriage are if for no other reason than the decision recognizes the humanity of gay men and women and that they are entitled to equal protection under our laws as citizens of the United States.

At the end of the day, gay marriage is not about you or me or what we think is right and wrong. Gay marriage is about the dignity and respect our fellow Americans deserve as citizens of the United States and equality under the law exactly like the way we have extended dignity and respect, under the law at least, to African Americans, Jewish Americans, Asian Americans, women and the disabled.

Gay Issues in Flux

In terms of gay marriage issues, the United States is behind other nations of the world. . . .

The campaign for a constitutional amendment banning gay marriage in the United States is a young one, but very reflective of modern society in the United States and the culture war that exists between liberal and traditional or conservative values. Over the last two decades, various state and federal court decisions have called attention to the issue of same-sex marriage. These decisions have been reported in the media, but they have had minimal impact on the nation's public psyche—much like the notice most Californians pay to numerous minor earthquakes that occasionally remind them that the ground they walk on is actually a geologically active planet.

But in late 2003 the Massachusetts Supreme Court—in a landmark ruling as earth-shattering as an 8.0 magnitude earthquake—decided that laws prohibiting gay marriage were unconstitutional, thus opening the door for gay men and women to legally marry for the first time in the United States. This ruling drew immediate attacks from those opposed to gay marriage and resulted in an attempt to pass an amendment to the United States Constitution that would restrict marriage in all states to be between a man and a woman. The issue polarized America and became a major campaign issue in the 2004 election cycle. George W. Bush used the same-sex marriage issue to eke out a narrow re-election to the Presidency over Senator John Kerry from Massachusetts.

The Fourteenth Amendment to the U.S. Constitution is generally the keystone to any civil rights argument.

With California's Proposition 8 and the constitutional status of same-sex marriage in California along with the recent repeal of the military's "Don't Ask, Don't Tell" policy, a review of DOMA and First Amendment hate speech protection currently making headlines as they progress through various court systems, issues regarding the status of homosexual men and women as citizens of the United States and the rights and privileges that they are entitled to along with the dignity the rest of the United States citizenry accords them will remain in flux until these issues are ultimately resolved by the United States Supreme Court.

The Legal Issues

In many ways, the issues that homosexuals and same-sex couples are facing now are the same civil rights issues resolved by the Supreme Court in *Brown v. Board of Education*. While domestic partnerships and civil unions convey some of the rights to marriage heterosexual couples enjoy, they are widely viewed as a contractual expedience rather than the state-sanctioned institution connoted by the word "marriage." This relegates the emotional bond and love that committed same-sex couples share to second-class status in a nation where the traditional family unit of man, woman, and children reigns supreme. In *Brown*, the Supreme Court ruled that separate, but equal in terms of racial segregation, was unconstitutional under the Fourteenth Amendment's equal protection clause. A tsunami of civil rights legislation and reform followed the *Brown* decision. The question now, is, will the Supreme Court ultimately decide that heterosexual marriage and same-sex civil unions are another unconstitutional instance of separateness and inequality. When they do, without a constitutional amendment specifically prohibiting it, same-sex marriage will likely be found constitutional under the Fourteenth Amendment.

The Fourteenth Amendment to the U.S. Constitution is generally the keystone to any civil rights argument. Ratified in 1868 after the Civil War, the Fourteenth Amendment has been used to end segregation and legalize abortion. The relevant portion of the amendment reads: "No State shall make or enforce any law which shall abridge the privileges or immunities of citizens of the United States; nor shall any State deprive any person of life, liberty, or property, without due process of law; nor deny to any person within its jurisdiction the equal protection of the laws."

Both the clauses: "equal protection of the laws," and "nor shall any State deprive any person of life, liberty, or property;" are in play in regards to the issue of same-sex marriage. In

Loving v. Virginia the Supreme Court unanimously ruled that the Commonwealth of Virginia's "Racial Integrity Act," which required a citizen's race to be recorded and made it a felony to marry outside one's race, was unconstitutional on the grounds that it violated the equal protection clause of the Fourteenth Amendment. Writing the opinion for the court, chief Justice Earl Warren wrote that "the Fourteenth Amendment requires that the freedom of choice to marry not be restricted by invidious racial discrimination. Under our Constitution, the freedom to marry, or not marry, a person of another race resides with the individual and cannot be infringed on by the State."

In 1992, voters in Colorado saw what the *Loving v. Virginia* ruling might imply for same-sex marriages, so they attempted to amend the Colorado Constitution in a way that would ban same-sex marriage if gays and lesbians were indeed categorized as a minority. . . .

The Amendment was never enacted as a District Court judge approved an injunction against the law, and the Colorado Supreme Court overruled it on the grounds that it violated the Fourteenth Amendment when "strict scrutiny" was applied.

The State of Colorado appealed to the U.S. Supreme Court in *Romer v. Evans*, and the Court voted 6-3 that the U.S. Constitution's Fourteenth Amendment supersedes the Colorado Constitution and that Amendment 2 was so broadly hostile to a minority group that there was no compelling state interest to enact it. . . .

In [*Romer*] . . . Kennedy invokes the Fourteenth Amendment's equal protection clause specifically. Additionally, while he refers to homosexuals as a "certain class," and as a "group of citizens," he stops short in *Romer*, of labeling homosexuals as a "suspect class." In *Lawrence v. Texas*, Justice Sandra Day O'Connor and Kennedy again stop short of labeling homosexuals a "suspect class." This is significant for what is not said. For at the same time the court recognizes that homosexuals are entitled to equal protection under the law, they choose to be very careful that their opinions will be worded so that they do not specifically construe a right to marriage. For if homosexuals are regarded as a suspect class under the Fourteenth Amendment, then any legal decisions regarding due process of law and equal protection under the law would have to be applied with a "strict scrutiny" standard instead of a "rational scrutiny" standard. It was through the application of "strict scrutiny" that the court unanimously ruled that separate but equal was unconstitutional under the Fourteenth Amendment in *Brown*.

It would appear that the Supreme Court believes that the definition of marriage as one man married to one woman may be needlessly discriminatory.

But *Lawrence* was significant for another reason in that the court ruled that morality cannot override civil liberties. Lori Watson, in her essay "Constituting Politics: Power, Reciprocity, and Identity," explains that homosexuals, and women, constitute what can be described as "dominated groups" under John Rawls' theory of social justice and political liberalism. Her essay examines the struggles of dominated groups in forming identities when political structures place these groups at disadvantages. Watson explains that membership in a socially dominated group transforms one's status as citizen, as evidenced by Justice Scalia's dissent in *Lawrence v. Texas* (2003). Watson concludes that for citizens to be free and equal, political structures in place that dominate other groups based on gender, race and sexual orientation need to be dismantled.

In *Lawrence* the Supreme Court ruled that consensual sex acts within the home are protected by a right to privacy. Many states have laws on the books outlawing sodomy and even fornication outside of marriage under any circumstances. However, in *Griswold v. Connecticut* and *Eisenstadt v. Baird*, the Supreme Court ruled that the decision to have children was fundamental and immune to government intrusion. Previously, in *Bowers v. Hardwick* the Court upheld a Georgia law banning sodomy between two consenting males, citing America's aversion to homosexuality as a reasonable basis for not extending protection to homosexual sex. In deciding *Lawrence* however, the Court overruled their previous decision in *Bowers* and held that the Texas law did not contain a compelling state interest that justified the intrusion into Mr. Lawrence's home.

A Concern for Basic Human Dignity

Given the above Supreme Court decisions, it would appear that the Supreme Court believes that the definition of marriage as one man married to one woman may be needlessly discriminatory, and if so, a legal argument for same-sex marriage may be emerging; and yet, the court is very carefully navigating the legal minefield so that their decisions cannot be construed to articulate a constitutional right to same-sex marriage:

- In *Loving* the Supreme Court ruled that the decision to marry is a fundamental right that resides with the individual, not the state.

- In *Romer*, the Supreme Court ruled that the state cannot discriminate against homosexuals.

- In *Lawrence* the Supreme Court held that morality could not be the factor that overrides one's civil liberties.

Loving, Romer, and *Lawrence* set the stage for *Goodridge v. Department of Public Health* in which the Massachusetts Supreme Court held that the State does not have a rational basis to deny same-sex couples marriage under the equal protection and due process clauses of the Fourteenth Amendment. The court found that the state may not "deny the protections, benefits and obligations conferred by civil marriage to two individuals of the same sex who wish to marry." Chief Justice Margaret Marshall, writing for the majority, wrote that the state's constitution "affirms the dignity and equality of all individuals. It forbids the creation of second-class citizens," that the state had no "constitutionally adequate reason for denying marriage to same-sex couples," and "the right to marry is not a privilege conferred by the State, but a fundamental right that is protected against unwarranted State interference." ...

The Role of Federalism

Another major factor in any ultimate decision by the United States Supreme Court in ruling same-sex marriage constitutional under the Fourteenth Amendment is the role of federalism in practice by the states. Federalism is a double-edged sword. According to Gary Gerstle, professor of American history at Vanderbilt University, "many gay marriage and marijuana legalization advocates now believe that they can accomplish more in state rather than national arenas." His essay, "Federalism in America: Beyond the Tea Partiers" suggests that the true power of federalism is in the use of the states as laboratories for public policy to find more nimble solutions to pressing social issues than the United States central government is capable of.

The states are indeed a laboratory for public policy. As of February 2011, there are 41 states with explicit bans on gay marriage, most passed within the past four years. Same-sex marriage is legal in three states as a result of court rulings and in two others—as well as the District of Columbia—through votes in their respective legislatures. As of February 2011, same-sex marriages were granted in Connecticut, Iowa, Massachusetts, New Hampshire, Vermont, and Washington, D.C., along with the Coquille Indian Tribe in Oregon. Same-sex marriage licenses were available in California between June 16,

2008, and November 4, 2008. Civil unions are legally recognized in California, Colorado, Hawaii, Maine, Maryland, Nevada, Oregon, Rhode Island, Wisconsin, Illinois and Washington. Oregon, Washington, Hawaii, the District of Columbia and Maine have domestic partnership laws granting gay couples varying degrees of spousal rights. Arkansas gays and unmarried straight couples are banned from adopting or fostering children.

As each state adopts its own policies and imposes its own bans or grants privileges, different issues will arise that will certainly generate legal action. Perhaps there is no better example of the tangled web quagmire than what has resulted with Proposition 8 in California. Proposition 8 overturned a California Supreme Court ruling that had allowed same-sex marriages in California. As predicted, Proposition 8 was quickly challenged in and overturned in federal court. The case was appealed to the Ninth Circuit Court in *Perry v. Schwarzenegger*, and is pending. The Circuit Court decision is sure to be appealed to the Supreme Court. When the appeal is made, the [Chief Justice John] Roberts [US Supreme] Court, with three female justices, including Ruth Bader Ginsburg, will have an opportunity to make a landmark decision.

Recent decisions in the state and federal court systems indicate that an ultimate showdown before the Supreme Court is inevitable.

It's possible that marriage will be seen as a fundamental individual right and that the state cannot remove that right without showing a compelling state interest that is not solely based on concepts of morality. Unless opponents of same-sex marriage can provide a new and compelling argument opposing same-sex marriage, they are only left with the popular-majority argument (which was overruled in *Loving*) and the morality argument (which was overruled in *Lawrence*). With no legal argument left, the Supreme Court would ultimately conclude that same-sex marriage bans are needlessly discriminatory and unconstitutional.

Such a ruling is well within the realm of possibility. At the end of the last Supreme Court session in 2010, *The New York Times* reported on an apparently innocent statement from Justice Ruth Bader Ginsburg, writing for the majority in *Christian Legal Society v. Martinez, Martinez* revolved around "whether a public law school could deny recognition to a student group that excluded gay men and lesbians." Ginsburg said: "Our decisions have declined to distinguish between status and conduct in this context." But the context is what mattered. Justice Ginsburg, writing for the majority, was talking about laws affecting gay men and lesbians. Columbia Law Professor Suzanne B. Goldberg believes that Ginsburg's statement is reflective of the much larger issue of suspect class status. Goldberg believes that "the court is talking about gay people, not homosexuals, and about people who have a social identity rather than a class of people who engage in particular sex acts," which is really at the heart of the dignity and citizen status of homosexuals and behind the heterosexual need to keep the linguistic term "marriage" to themselves. If this is indeed the case, then equal protection and due process of law under the Fourteenth Amendment would most definitely apply to homosexuals and same-sex marriage the same way it does in *Brown* and *Loving*. But until the negative moral perceptions of perceived homosexual acts meliorates and becomes more widely accepted, any Supreme Court decision of the magnitude Goldberg suggests will be severely criticized by the traditional and conservative segments of United States citizenry. . . .

While defining issues and outcomes through the court system can be a very long and winding process, recent decisions in the state and federal court systems indicate that an ultimate showdown before the Supreme Court is inevitable. When that day comes, homosexuals and same-sex couples will likely achieve full status as citizens, and same-sex marriage will likely be found constitutional under the Fourteenth Amendment. When that day comes we will take a giant step forward as a civil society that respects the rights and dignities of not only our fellow Americans, but of all humanity.

13

A Constitutional Amendment Is Needed to Save Traditional Marriage

Bill Frist

Bill Frist was the US Senate majority leader in 2006.

Although same-sex marriage is legal in several states, many more states have amended their constitutions to limit marriage to heterosexual couples. But unless a federal marriage amendment is passed, activist courts may force states to accept gay marriage. Bill Frist discusses his plan to bring the Marriage Protection Amendment to the Senate floor in 2006. He claims that the Marriage Protection Amendment has nothing to do with discriminating against same-sex couples, but instead is about preserving traditional marriage that has served society well throughout history.

Throughout history, the union between a man and woman has been recognized and honored as an essential cornerstone of society. Customs come and go and vary by time and place, but the institution of marriage has endured through millennia.

On Monday, June 5, I will bring to the Senate floor the Marriage Protection Amendment to ensure the definition of marriage endures and remains true to the wishes of the majority of the American people.

Marriage Protection Amendment

The amendment reads simply: "Marriage in the United States shall consist only of the union of a man and a woman. Neither this Constitution, nor the constitution of any State, shall be construed to require that marriage or the legal incidents thereof be conferred upon any union other than the union of a man and a woman."

Preserving traditional marriage is a matter of safeguarding the well-being of our children, our country and our future.

Tennessee, which will give voters the opportunity to voice their opinions on the sanctity of marriage this November, is one of seven states with similar amendments to their constitutions pending. Already 45 states have approved legislation that defines marriage as a union between a man and woman, and no state has ever rejected an effort to protect traditional marriage when it has been on the ballot.

Citizens in these states understand that radically redefining the institution of marriage is social engineering on a massive scale. Preserving traditional marriage is a matter of safeguarding the well-being of our children, our country and our future. It is certainly not a matter that should be decided by liberal, activist judges who choose to legislate from the bench without regard for the public's will.

But this is exactly what is happening. There are currently nine states whose laws or amendments protecting traditional marriage are under court challenge. Just last year, the state of Nebraska saw its democratically enacted amendment to protect traditional marriage, which passed with 70% of the vote, struck down by an unelected federal judge with a lifetime appointment.

And earlier this month, a state marriage amendment approved by over 76% of Georgia voters was thrown out by a judge on a technicality. Georgia's voters passed the amendment to guard against just such an occurrence, believing a state constitutional amendment to be harder to strike down than an almost identically worded law passed by the state legislature in 1996.

Such judicial activism constitutes a blatant thwarting of the public's will and the common good. Given these circumstances, to say that marriage is under attack is not an overstatement. The best way to protect state laws from reversal is to enact a constitutional amendment that defines marriage as being between one man and one woman.

The Marriage Protection Amendment has nothing to do with discriminating against same-sex couples and everything to do with preserving for future generations the fundamental institution that has sustained society throughout history. Courts should not be allowed to suppress the voices and votes of the American people by permanently redefining marriage in America.

14

A Constitutional Amendment Against Gay Marriage Would Restrict Liberty

National Organization for Women (NOW)

National Organization for Women (NOW) is an organization of feminist activists that works to bring about equality for all women.

A number of states have either passed gay marriage laws or are considering doing so, but many other states still ban same-sex marriage. Both gay and heterosexual couples should have the protections and benefits afforded by marriage, including Social Security benefits, healthcare, disability, and favorable estate tax treatment, and allowing civil same-sex marriages will accomplish this. The Federal Marriage Amendment, however, would deny same-sex couples these basic rights and protections. If successful, the amendment would mark the first time the United States amended its constitution to restrict rather than expand liberty. This article has been edited from the original and only excerpts, rather than the full article, have been reprinted.

Marriage equality is a reality in the District of Columbia and six states—Connecticut, Iowa, Massachusetts, New Hampshire, New York and Vermont. The state of Maryland recognizes same-sex marriages performed in jurisdictions where it is legal. It's important to note, however, that 41 states still have statutes or constitutional amendments banning marriage for same-sex couples.

In California, same-sex marriage was legal for six months in 2008 until Proposition 8 passed, restricting the right to marry in the state to opposite-sex couples. The decision by the California State Supreme Court to uphold Proposition 8 and reinstate discrimination against same-sex couples was a devastating setback on the march to equality. The legal battle continues in California, and NOW [the National Organization for Women] will continue to be in the streets in communities across the nation until marriage equality for same-sex couples is recognized in every state.

Feminism

The struggle for equal marriage rights is a feminist issue. Women will not achieve full equality until every woman can pursue her dreams free from discrimination. NOW declared full support for same-sex marriage in 1995, claiming that the choice of marriage is a fundamental constitutional right under the equal protection clause of the 14th Amendment that should not be denied because of a person's sexual orientation.

Feminism is rooted in freedom, independence and love. Lesbian women should be able to marry their partner and be entitled to the same rights as their heterosexual sisters.

The right wing is telling women they have to marry a man in order to get married—holding relationships of women with men on a pedestal. Not allowing women to marry other women promotes a patriarchal society where women's economic security is dependent on their relationship with men.

Feminism is about having choices and opportunities. Women are free to choose a partner and should have the opportunity to marry or not marry their partner regardless of gender.

Civil Rights

The right to marry has been recognized by the Supreme Court as a fundamental right under the United States Constitution.

Government has no business intruding in our personal lives. A Constitutional amendment to ban same-sex marriages would write discrimination into the Constitution.

All couples, lesbian and gay and heterosexual, deserve the legal protections afforded by marriage. Currently, same-sex couples in committed relationships are likely to pay higher taxes than married couples. They receive no Social Security survivor benefits upon the death of a partner despite paying payroll taxes. They are denied healthcare, disability, military and other benefits afforded to heterosexual couples. Without a will, they often pay estate taxes when a partner dies, including significant tax penalties when they inherit a 401K pension plan from a partner. They are denied family leave under the Family and Medical Leave Act.

Civil marriage will give same-sex couples the same economic security, protections and peace of mind that is enjoyed by heterosexual married couples.

Children of same-sex couples are penalized by marriage discrimination. More than 1 million children are currently being raised by same-sex couples in the United States, according to the 2000 census. Many lesbian and gay parents, however, are unable to assume full legal parenting rights and responsibilities, and in most states, there is no law guaranteeing a non-custodial, biological or adoptive parent's visitation rights or requiring child support from such a parent. Without the ability to establish a legal relationship to both parents, these children are left without protections such as Social Security survivor benefits.

Writing discrimination into the constitution, federal or state, is unjust. It singles out a group of people and categorizes them as less than others undeserving of legal and economic protections and second-class citizens. Marriage discrimination subjects same-sex couples to the tyranny of the majority. . . .

Marriage Benefits

Civil marriage will give same-sex couples the same economic security, protections and peace of mind that is enjoyed by heterosexual married couples.

[The Federal Marriage Amendment] is a harsh, discriminatory measure that would prevent same-sex couples . . . from having any basic rights and protections under the law.

There are 400 state benefits and 1,100+ federal benefits granted to married couples. Here are just a few:

- Access to employer-provided health and retirement benefits for partner and nonbiological/adoptive children.

- Access to partner's coverage under Medicare and Social Security.

- Ability to visit or make medical decisions for an ill or incapacitated partner.

- Right to sue for wrongful death of partner.

- Ability to sponsor one's partner for immigration.

- Marital children gain family stability and economic security because of their parents' legal marriage that is inaccessible to nonmarital children, including the enhanced approval of marital children in society and streamlined adoption processes.

- Access to health benefits and inheritance from both parents.

- Right to maintain a relationship with the non-biological/adoptive parent in the event of the death of one parent (in states without same-sex second-parent adoptions).

- Joint insurance policies for home, auto and health.

- Joint parenting and Joint adoption.

- Bereavement or sick leave to care for a partner or child.

Continue to Oppose a Federal Marriage Amendment

The Federal Marriage Amendment [FMA] would ban any protections under the law for same-sex couples. The amendment goes much farther than simply defining marriage as a union between a man and a woman. This is a harsh, discriminatory measure that would prevent same-sex couples who have made commitments to each other from having any basic rights and protections under the law.

Right-wing propagandists continue to pass legislation that will write discrimination and bigotry into the U.S. Constitution to prevent equal marriage rights. Throughout history, the U.S. Constitution has been used to ensure, protect and expand the individual liberties of all people in the United States. The FMA would restrict rights, not expand them.

The anti-gay amendments to the U.S. Constitution and the States' Constitution are intended to define marriage as the "union between a man and a woman" and designed to deny same-sex couples ANY legal protections.

The Federal Marriage Amendment would write discrimination in the Constitution. The U.S. Constitution was written to protect and ensure equal treatment for ALL. This amendment would destroy that equality by rewriting the Constitution to treat one group of people different from others. Since the Bill of Rights was passed, there have been only 17 amendments to the Constitution, and these amendments have expanded people's rights—such as giving African-Americans and women the right to vote. The Federal Marriage Amendment would be the first time in history that the Constitution was amended to restrict the rights of a group of people. . . .

Cultural Perspective

It was once illegal in many states for people of different races to marry. Just as we ended legal discrimination based on race, we should end discrimination against lesbians, gays, bisexual and transgender people.

Lesbian and gay couples want to marry for the same reasons as heterosexual couples. No good reason exists for excluding same-sex couples from the protections and responsibilities of marriage.

Civil marriage for gays and lesbians affirms the institution and importance of marriage. Marriage is about love and commitment. Heterosexual love is not superior to homosexual love and vice versa. Partnerships should be held equally under the law regardless of the gender of the people in them.

With changing norms and cultural diversity, our society is changing quickly and the definition of a family has to change with the times to recognize lesbian and gay families. Allowing same-sex couples to marry shows our commitment to diversity, equality, tolerance and respect.

There are many stereotypes surrounding same-sex relationships. Homosexuals and their relationships are often judged as a promiscuous and only about sex. These stereotypes need to be recognized and addressed. Lesbian and gay relationships (like heterosexual relationships) are about love and commitment. People who love each other and care about fairness and justice can fight for the equality of all people and support equal marriage.

The institution of marriage is not static and has changed significantly over time. Married women used to be the legal property of their husbands, Asian immigrants were prohibited from marrying each other, and interracial marriages were prohibited by anti-miscegenation laws. A strong institution accommodates social and cultural shifts. Granting the LGBT community the right to marry is simply the evolution of human rights.

Why Not Civil Unions Instead of Marriage?

Allowing same-sex couples civil marriage rights opens up marriage to more people and does not redefine religious marriage in our society.

Separate is not equal. Marriage equality is a fundamental right. Same-sex couples cannot participate fully in our society if they are denied the legal rights and cultural privileges offered to heterosexual couples through marriage.

Children benefit from legal marriage. One thing that both sides of the marriage issue can agree on is that marriage strengthens families—children are more secure if they are raised by two loving parents who have a legal relationship with them and can share the responsibility of parenthood equally as well as gaining the cultural acceptance of legal marriage.

Civil unions and domestic partnerships are no substitute for civil marriage. Though an important advance in the fight for equality, civil unions and domestic partnerships do not carry the full legal benefits (especially government and tax benefits) or cultural significance of marriage. The substitution of civil unions for legal marriage assigns same-sex couples to second class status—separate and unequal.

Civil unions only grant couples *state* benefits. Also, states differ in their eligibility rules for civil unions and states can decide whether or not to recognize civil unions at all. Civil unions do not provide couples with any *federal* benefits.

Conservative Arguments

Allowing lesbian and gay couples to get legally married does not threaten nor take away rights from married heterosexual couples. Granting the LGBT community to marry does not weaken or destroy the marriage of heterosexuals.

Conservatives claim there is a need to "defend marriage." Marriage is not under attack. If marriage was under attack, the LGBT community would be rebelling against marriage instead of fighting for the right to marry.

Anti-LGBT activists armed with empty sound bites—like "activist judges" and "protecting or defending marriage"—are trying to obscure the real impact of these pernicious amendments and ballot initiatives that are attacking millions of families.

Some conservatives and religious fundamentalists argue because heterosexuals can procreate they should be entitled to marriage. Many heterosexuals cannot or do not wish to procreate. Should we ban them from marrying? Of course not because marriage is not about procreation—it is about love and commitment between two people.

Some conservatives argue that gay marriage should not be allowed because homosexuality is unnatural. Conservatives made this argument thirty years ago as well when opposing interracial marriage. And who gets to say what is natural and what it is not? Right-wing conservatives argue lesbian and gay rights are special rights. Since only approximately 10% of the nation cannot marry (the LGBT community) then it would seem heterosexuals are the ones with special rights since they have the right to marry.

Religious Freedom

The issue of marriage equality is also an issue of religious freedom. The struggle for same-sex marriage is about legal rights—it does not demand that any church perform same-sex marriage ceremonies. However, the government fails to ensure religious freedom when it refuses to honor the unions of same-sex couples performed by one religion in the same way it honors those of opposite-sex couples.

Religious groups do not have to recognize civil marriages. Churches and other religious institutions would not have to recognize or perform ceremonies for these marriages. Some religious groups recognize lesbian and gay couples and others do not—government should not interfere with religion or impose one religion's beliefs on people who hold different beliefs.

The United States was founded on the principle of separation of church and state. The government of the United States has no right to discriminate against the LGBT community because of a religious belief. If the government does base an amendment on religion to discriminate, governments will be favoring one religion over another because many religions support same-sex marriage.

Organizations to Contact

The editors have compiled the following list of organizations concerned with the issues debated in this book. The descriptions are derived from materials provided by the organizations. All have publications or information available for interested readers. The list was compiled on the date of publication of the present volume; the information provided here may change. Be aware that many organizations take several weeks or longer to respond to inquiries, so allow as much time as possible.

American Civil Liberties Union (ACLU)
125 Broad Street, 18th Floor, New York, NY   10004
(212) 549-2500
e-mail: media@aclu.org
website: www.aclu.org

The ACLU is the nation's oldest and largest civil liberties organization. Its Lesbian Gay Bisexual and Transgender Project, started in 1986, fights discrimination and advocates on behalf of lesbians, gays, bisexuals, and transgender individuals in the courts, legislatures, and public education. It focuses on five issue areas: Relationships, Youth & Schools, Parenting, Gender Identity and Expression, Discrimination in Employment, and Housing. One of the Project's goals is to obtain full legal recognition of LGBT relationships through domestic partnerships, civil unions and, ultimately, marriage.

Canadian Lesbian and Gay Archives
34 Isabella Street, Toronto, Ontario   M4Y 1N1
  Canada
(416) 777-2755
e-mail: queeries@clga.ca
website: http://clga.ca

This organization collects and maintains information and materials relating to the gay and lesbian rights movement in Canada and elsewhere. Its collection of records and other materials documenting the stories of lesbians and gay men and their organizations in Canada is available to the public for education and research. It also publishes an annual newsletter, *Lesbian and Gay Archivist.*

Children of Gays and Lesbians Everywhere (COLAGE)
1550 Bryant Street, Suite 830, San Francisco, CA 94103
(415) 861-5437
e-mail: colage@colage.org
website: www.colage.org

COLAGE supports gay marriage on the grounds that it would be good for children. It is a national and international organization that supports young people with lesbian, gay, bisexual, and transgender (LGBT) parents. Its mission is to foster the growth of daughters and sons of LGBT parents by providing education, support, and community.

Concerned Women for America (CWFA)
1015 15th St. NW, Suite 1100, Washington, DC 20005
(202) 488-7000 • fax: (202) 488-0806
e-mail: mail@cwfa.org
website: www.cwfa.org

The CWFA is an educational and legal defense foundation that seeks to strengthen the traditional family by promoting Judeo-Christian moral standards. It opposes gay marriage and the granting of additional civil rights protections to gays and lesbians. The CWFA publishes the monthly magazine *Family Voice* and various position papers on gay marriage and other issues.

Family Research Council (FRC)
801 G St. NW, Washington, DC 20001
(202) 393-2100 • fax: (202) 393-2134
website: www.frc.org

The Family Research Council is a research, resource, and educational organization that promotes the traditional family, which it defines as a group of people bound by marriage, blood, or adoption. It opposes gay marriage and adoption rights and publishes numerous reports from a conservative perspective on issues affecting the family, including homosexuality and same-sex marriage.

Family Research Institute (FRI)

PO Box 62640, Colorado Springs, CO   80962-2640
(303) 681-3113
website: www.familyresearchinst.org

The FRI distributes information about family, sexuality, and substance abuse issues. It believes that strengthening marriage would reduce many social problems, including crime, poverty, and sexually transmitted diseases. The institute publishes the bimonthly newsletter *Family Research Report* as well numerous position papers and opinion articles.

Focus on the Family

8605 Explorer Drive, Colorado Springs, CO   80920
(800) 232-6459
website: www.focusonthefamily.com

Focus on the Family is a conservative Christian organization that promotes traditional family values and gender roles. Its publications include the monthly magazine *Focus on the Family* and the numerous anti-gay marriage reports and articles.

Gay and Lesbian Advocates and Defenders (GLAD)

30 Winter Street, Suite 800, Boston, MA   02108
(617) 426-1350 • fax: (617) 426-3594
e-mail: gladlaw@glad.org
website: www.glad.org

GLAD is a legal rights organization that is dedicated to ending discrimination based on sexual orientation, HIV status and gender identity and expression. GLAD was a major supporter of same-sex marriage legalization in Connecticut, Massachusetts, New Hampshire, Maine, and Vermont.

Lambda Legal Defense and Education Fund, Inc.
120 Wall Street, 19th Floor, New York, NY 10005
(212) 809-8585 • fax: (212) 809-0055
website: www.lambdalegal.org

Lambda is a public-interest law firm committed to achieving full recognition of the civil rights of homosexuals. The firm addresses a variety of areas, including equal marriage rights, the military, parenting and relationship issues, and domestic-partner benefits. It publishes the quarterly *Lambda Update* and the pamphlet *Freedom to Marry*.

National Center for Lesbian Rights
870 Market Street, Suite 370, San Francisco, CA 94102
(415) 392-6257 • fax: (415) 392-8442
website: www.nclrights.org

The center is a public-interest law office that provides legal counseling and representation for victims of sexual-orientation discrimination. Primary areas of advice include child custody and parenting, employment, housing, the military, and insurance. The center has a section devoted to marriage rights for lesbians and gays.

National Gay and Lesbian Task Force (NGLTF)
1325 Massachusetts Ave. NW, Suite 600
Washington, DC 20005
(202) 393-5177 • fax: (202) 393-2241
website: www.thetaskforce.org

NGLTF is a civil-rights advocacy organization that lobbies Congress and the White House on a range of civil rights issues. The organization is working to make same-sex marriage legal. It publishes numerous papers and pamphlets, and the booklet *To Have and to Hold: Organizing for Our Right to Marry* and the fact sheet "Lesbian and Gay Families."

National Organization for Marriage
2029 K Street NW, Suite 300, Washington, DC   20006
(888) 894-3604 • fax: (888) 894-3604
e-mail: contact@nationformarriage.org
website: www.nationformarriage.org

This organization's mission is to protect marriage and the religious communities that sustain it. It was founded in 2007 in response to the growing movement to legalize same-sex marriage in state legislatures. It publishes numerous fact sheets, reports, and other articles on why same-sex marriage should not be legalized.

Pew Forum on Religion & Public Life
1615 L Street NW, Suite 700, Washington, DC   20036-5610
(202) 419-4550 • fax: (202) 419-4559
Web site: http://pewforum.org

The Pew Forum on Religion & Public Life is a project of the Pew Research Center, a nonpartisan "fact tank" that provides information on the issues, attitudes, and trends shaping America and the world. The Pew Forum studies various aspects of religion and public life in the United States and around the world, and provides a neutral venue for discussing issues in this area.

Bibliography

Books

Gordon A. Babst, Emily R. Gill, and Jason Pierceson	*Moral Argument, Religion, and Same-Sex Marriage: Advancing the Public Good*, Lanham, MD: Lexington Books, 2009.
M.V. Lee Badgett	*When Gay People Get Married: What Happens When Societies Legalize Same-Sex Marriage*, New York: New York University Press, 2009.
David Blankenhorn	*The Future of Marriage*, Jackson, TN: Encounter Books, 2009.
George Chauncey	*Why Marriage: The History Shaping Today's Debate Over Gay Equality*, New York: Basic Books, 2009.
David Orgon Coolidge, William C. Duncan, Mark Strasser and Lynn D. Wardle	*Marriage and Same-Sex Unions: A Debate*, Santa Barbara, CA: Praeger, 2008.
Evan Gerstmann	*Same-Sex Marriage and the Constitution*, Cambridge, MA: Cambridge University Press, 2008.
Patricia A. Gozemba	*History of America's First Legal Same-Sex Marriages*, Ypsilanti, MI: Beacon Press, 2007.

Frederick Hertz and Emily Doskow	*Making it Legal: A Guide to Same-Sex Marriage, Domestic Partnerships & Civil Unions*, Berkeley, CA: NOLO, 2011
Andrew Koppelman	*Same Sex, Different States: When Same-Sex Marriages Cross State Lines*, New Haven, CT: Yale University Press, 2006.
Sheri Lynne Lawson	*The Spell of Religion: And the Battle over Gay Marriage*, Parker, CO: Outskirts Press, 2009.
Man Yee Karen Lee	*Equality, Dignity, and Same-Sex Marriage: A Rights Disagreement in Democratic Societies*, Leiden, The Netherlands: Martinus Nijhoff Publishers, 2010.
Susan Gluck Mezey	*Gay Families and the Courts: The Quest for Equal Rights*, Lanham, MD: Rowman & Littlefield Publishers, 2009.
Nancy D. Polikoff and Michael Bronski	*Beyond (Straight and Gay) Marriage: Valuing All Families Under the Law*, Ypsilanti, MI: Beacon Press, 2009.
Peter Nicolas and Mike Strong	*The Geography of Love: Same-Sex Marriage & Relationship Recognition in America*, Seattle, WA: CreateSpace, 2011.
Gerald N. Rosenberg	*The Hollow Hope: Can Courts Bring About Social Change?*, Chicago, IL: University of Chicago Press, 2008.

Michael J.
Rosenfeld
The Age of Independence: Interracial Unions, Same-Sex Unions, and the Changing American Family, Cambridge, MA: Harvard University Press, 2007.

Andrew Sullivan
Same-Sex Marriage: Pro and Con, Vancouver, WA: Vintage, 2009.

Frank Turek
Correct, Not Politically Correct; How Same-Sex Marriage Hurts Everyone, Charlotte, NC: CrossExamined, 2008.

Lynn D. Wardle,
ed.
What's the Harm? Does Legalizing Same-Sex Marriage Really Harm Individuals, Families or Society? Lanham, MD: University Press of America, 2008.

Periodicals and Internet Sources

Associated Press
"Obama: Defense Of Marriage Act Should Be Repealed," *The Huffington Post,* July 19, 2011. www.huffingtonpost.com.

David Badash
"GOP Debate: Constitutional Ban On Same-Sex Marriage Wins Big," *The New Civil Rights Movement,* June 14, 2011. http://thenewcivilrights movement.com.

Bob Barr
"No Defending the Defense of Marriage Act," *Los Angeles Times,* January 5, 2009. www.latimes.com.

Michelle Boorstein

"Same-Sex Marriage Again an Issue for Religious Charities," *The Washington Post*, July 12, 2011. www.washingtonpost.com.

Philip N. Cohen

"Same-Sex Marriage and Children, What We Don't Know Shouldn't Hurt Us," *The Huffington Post*, April 10, 2009. www.huffingtonpost.com.

Nicholas Confessore

"Beyond New York, Gay Marriage Faces Hurdles," *New York Times*, June 26, 2011.

Cristen Conger

"Does a Parent's Gender Impact a Child's Success?," *Discovery News*, January 28, 2010. http://news .discovery.com.

Sara Israelsen-Hartley

"Traditional Marriage Has Impact Beyond Faith," *Deseret News*, January 27, 2011. www.deseretnews.com.

Chris Johnson

"2011 to Bring New Marriage Fights Across U.S.," *Washington Blade*, January 13, 2011. www.washington blade.com.

Ed Kilgore

"The Hypocrisy of 'States' rights' Conservatives: The 10th Amendment Is Sacred to the Right—Except When It Comes to Fighting Abortion and Gay Rights," *Salon*, August 7, 2011. www.salon.com.

Michal A. Lindenberger

"Why California's Gay-Marriage Ban Was Upended," *TIME*, August 5, 2010.

Adam Liptak   "Looking for Time Bombs and Tea
                       Leaves on Gay Marriage," *New York
                       Times*, July 20, 2010, p. A11.

Tom McFeely   "Needed: A Federal Marriage
                       Amendment," *National Catholic
                       Register*, April 17, 2009. www
                       .ncregister.com.

Jennifer Roback   "Same-Sex 'Marriage' and the
Morse   Persecution of Civil Society," *National
                       Catholic Register*, June 3, 2008.
                       www.ncregister.com.

Paul Mulshine   "Same-Sex Marriage: Right or
                       Wrong, It's Not a Right," NJ.com,
                       August 10, 2010. http://blog.nj.com.

Frank Newport   "For First Time, Majority of
                       Americans Favor Legal Gay Marriage:
                       Republicans and Older Americans
                       Remain Opposed," *Gallup*, May 20,
                       2011. www.gallup.com.

Martha   "A Right to Marry? Same-Sex
Nussbaum   Marriage and Constitutional Law,"
                       Dissent, Summer 2009. www.dissent
                       magazine.org.

Logan Penza   "Anti-Gay Marriage Movement =
                       Inefficiency," *The Moderate Voice*,
                       May 22, 2011. http://themoderate
                       voice.com.

Charlie Savage   "In Shift, U.S. Says Marriage Act
and Sheryl Gay   Blocks Gay Rights," *New York Times*,
Stolberg   February 23, 2011.

Erin Solaro   "Marriage Is a Human Right, Not a Religious Issue," *Seattle PI*, December 12, 2008. http://blog.seattlepi.com.

U.S. News &   "Is the Defense of Marriage Act
World Report   Constitutional? Debating Whether the Anti-Gay-Marriage Law Passes Muster," March 11, 2011. www .usnews.com.

Chrisopher Wolfe "What Marriage Has Become," *The Public Discourse*, March 21, 2011. www.thepublicdiscourse.com.

Index